Bible
·STORIES·

Bible ·STORIES·

TIGER BOOKS INTERNATIONAL LTD
LONDON

This edition published by
Tiger Books International Limited
3 Friars Lane, Richmond, Surrey, England

ISBN 1-870461-03-7

Designed by Clive Dorman
Typeset in Plantin by Paul Hicks Limited, Middleton, Manchester
Printed and bound in Yugoslavia by Grafoimpex

CONTENTS

Contents Continued

THE OLD TESTAMENT

THE GARDEN

LONG, long ago, in the very beginning of time, there was God.

There was no shape to the earth then, and total darkness and raging waters covered everything. Everywhere was waste and empty until God set about creating the world. He said "Let there be light", and the light came. God divided the light from the dark, and He called the light "Day" and the darkness "Night". Evening came and morning, and that was the first day.

Then God made the sky, like a great dome. Evening and morning came, and that was all done on the second day.

Next God made the earth. He ordered the waters below the sky to come together, and so it happened. He named the waters "Seas" and the dry land which was left He named "Earth", and He was pleased with what He saw. Then He ordered all kinds of plants to grow upon the earth—plants which bore grain and plants which bore fruit and plants with flowers. Evening and morning came, and that was the end of the third day.

Then God ordered great shining lights to appear in the sky. The two largest lights were the "Sun" and the "Moon"; the sun was to rule over the day, and the moon over the night. The smaller lights were the stars, including planets, comets and meteors. Evening and morning came, and so ended the fourth day.

However, there were as yet no living creatures in it. So the next day God made fish and birds. He filled the waters with all kinds of fish, from enormous sea-monsters and whales down to the tiniest minnows and sticklebacks.

In the air He put all kinds of birds, from great eagles to tiny wrens and linnets. The sea and the skies were now full of beautiful creatures. God was pleased with what He saw and He blessed all the living things He had made. When evening and morning had passed, that was the fifth day.

Then God said, "Let the earth produce all kinds of animals." He made a wonderful variety of creatures to live in the world; there were enormous beasts, like elephants, giraffes and rhinoceros, and tiny ones like moles and mice, shrews and spiders.

Then God said, "I will make human beings, who will be something like Me. They will take care of the fish, the birds and the animals, and all creatures which move in the sea and the sky, and on the earth."

So next He made a man, and breathed life-giving breath into him, and the man became a living soul. He was named Adam. God blessed him and placed him in the east of the world, in the beautiful Garden of Eden.

"You must have many children," God said, "so that they will grow and live all over the earh and look after it. You and they will be in charge of the fish, the birds and the animals."

Out of he ground God made grass and trees grow, and leafy plants for the animals and birds to eat; and He provided all kinds of grain and all kinds of fruit for people to eat—so that none would go hungry.

He looked at everything He had made and was pleased.

Evening and morning came, and that was the sixth day.

Now the universe was finished. God had completed His wonderful and flawless work.

So He stopped creating, and on the seventh day He rested. Then he blessed this seventh day and set it apart, and ever since then one day in seven has been a special day for people to rest from their work.

In the Garden of Eden, there grew all sorts of beautiful trees, which bore good fruit. A stream flowed through the garden to water it and, beyond Eden, this divided into four rivers; they were called the Pishon, the Gihon, the Tigris, and the Euphrates.

There were also two special trees in the middle of the garden. One was the Tree of Life and the other was the Tree of the Knowledge of Good and Evil.

When God put Adam in the Garden of Eden, He wanted him to cultivate it and take care of it, and so be a fellow-worker with Him. He said to Adam, "You may eat the fruit of any of the trees in the garden, except the fruit from the Tree of the Knowledge of Good and Evil. That fruit you must not eat; if you do then you will surely die."

Then God brought all the animals and birds in front of Adam, and Adam gave them all their names.

God had decided that it was not good for Adam to be all alone in the garden, so when Adam was alseep, He made a woman to share life in the garden with Adam.

Adam named her Eve, and they both began a happy life together looking after the beautiful garden and everything in it.

One of the creatures living in the garden was a snake, and he was very cunning. One day he glided up to Eve and said, "Did

God really say that you must not eat the fruit of any of the trees."

"No," replied Eve "we may eat the fruit from any of the trees, except from that tree in the middle—the tree which is called the Tree of the Knowledge of Good and Evil. God said that if we ate any of that fruit, then we would surely die."

"That's not true, you know," he hissed. "God said that because He knew that if you ate that fruit, then you would know all about good and evil, and so you would be like God Himself."

Eve looked at the beautiful tree again and saw how delicious its fruit looked. Perhaps a taste would not matter—and it would be wonderful to be as wise as God, she thought. It would do no harm if she took a bite. So she plucked one of the tempting fruits and ate it. It tasted nice, so she gave some to Adam and he ate too.

However, as soon as they had eaten, they suddenly realized what they had done and both felt very ashamed that they had disobeyed God. They knew they had chosen their own way and not God's, and that they had spoilt the beauty of that perfect garden by doing wrong. For the first time they became aware that they were naked and in their embarrassment they rushed to make clothing for themselves out of leaves.

That same evening, they heard God walking in the garden, but they felt guilty and tried to hide from Him among the trees.

But God called out, "Adam, where are you?"

"I heard You coming," answered Adam, "and I was afraid, so I hid myself from You."

'Have you eaten any of the fruit that I commanded you not to eat?" asked God.

"Eve gave the fruit to me and I ate it," said Adam, who was not feeling very brave and was ready to blame someone else.

God turned to Eve and said, "Why did you do this?"

Eve, too, tried to put the blame on to another, and she said, "The snake tricked me into it."

God was very sad at what had happened, for he felt that Adam and Eve could no longer be trusted and so were not fit to stay in the lovely garden. Their wrong-doing had to be punished.

Then He turned to the snake and said, "You, of all the animals, must bear the punishment for this. From now on you will have to crawl along the earth and eat the dust for as long as you live. You and the woman will always be enemies."

To Eve God said, "You will have to suffer pain when your children are born." And to Adam He said, "You listened to your wife and you ate the fruit which I had forbidden you to eat. Because of this you will have to work hard all your life to make the earth produce enough food for you. There will always be weeds and thorns and you will have to toil all the time to make anything grow on the land at all."

So where before Adam had been looking after a perfect and fertile garden, now he would have to struggle in a wilderness of weeds and thistles.

Then God said, "Now man has become like Me and has knowledge of good and evil. He cannot be allowed to eat the fruit of the Tree of Life also and thus live forever."

So God sent Adam and Eve out of the Garden of Eden, and Adam was set to work to cultivate the land outside it.

In order to keep either Adam and Eve, or anyone else, from coming near the Tree of Life, God placed winged creatures as a symbol of His majesty and presence at the east of the garden, and also angels, with a flaming sword, to keep out intruders.

NOAH AND THE FLOOD

LONG after Adam's time, when the world was full of people, God saw what a wicked and evil place it had become. He was sad. He felt sorry He had made such a beautiful world, filled with wonderful living creatures, if people were going to spoil it all by their wickedness.

However, there was one man with whom God was very pleased. He was a good man and his thoughts and deeds were noble and right. His name was Noah.

One day God said to Noah, "I have decided that this evil on earth cannot continue. A new start must be made; therefore a great flood will come which will destroy the wicked. Build yourself a boat—an ark—out of good timber; cover it with tar both inside and out, and make rooms inside it and a roof over it. Make three decks and put a door in the side. Then, when the flood comes, you and your wife and your sons and their wives will all be safe in the boat."

Probably Noah found this news rather startling, but he knew that he must do as God had said. He told his three sons, named Shem, Ham and Japheth, that they would have to help him with the building of his big boat so that it would be ready in time.

God had told him to make it 146 yards long, 24 yards wide, and 42 feet high. Moreover, as well as taking all the Noah family into

14

the ark, God said that Noah was also to take two of every kind of living creature—birds, animals and creeping things—in order to keep them alive, and there was to be a male and a female of each so that they would be able to reproduce again on the earth when the floods had gone, for there would be nothing else left alive.

Lastly God reminded Noah, "Take all kinds of food with you into the ark, both for you and for all the living creatures, for in seven days' time the rains will start, and it will rain for forty days and forty nights without stopping and you will not be able to leave the ark."

Noah did everything exactly as God had told him.

With the building of the ark finished, Noah had a thoroughly waterproof new home. Then he and his family began to round up all the animals and birds and insects and reptiles, as God had directed, and together they all went into the ark. Lastly Noah and his wife, and Shem, Ham, Japheth and their wives went into the ark themselves, and the door was firmly closed behind them. Then they settled down to watch the weather and wait for the promised rain. No doubt their actions were viewed with great amusement by those who saw the building of the ark. However, Noah's faith in God was justified.

Seven days later, just as God had said, it began to rain; and it rained in torrents, never stopping, for forty whole days and forty whole nights. The waters rose higher and higher, and the floods covered the whole earth, drowning every living thing. There was nothing left alive in the world except Noah, his family and the animals in his keeping.

Noah looked out upon the world he had known, and could see nothing but water, no matter which way he looked. All the land

and the trees and the places where people had lived were covered. Everything was being swamped by the flood waters. But God had promised Noah that he and his family would be saved, and Noah knew that God could be trusted.

The water was now deep enough for the ark to float, and as it became even deeper, the ark began to drift about on the surface.

Noah could not tell where they were, for the floods had risen so high that they had covered every part of the land. They went on rising so much that soon they were seven and a half yards above the tops of the highest mountains. There was nothing to be seen in any direction except water.

And they stayed like that for 150 days and nights. It must have seemed a very long time.

Then a great wind began to blow, and at last the waters started to go down. The rains stopped and gradually, for another 150 days, the waters began to go lower and lower. The ark stopped rocking to and fro, and at last it came to rest on a mountain called Ararat.

The waters continued to go down and one day, when Noah looked out, he found that he could see the tops of other mountains.

Noah waited for another forty days. Then he opened a window in the ark and let a raven fly out. It flew around for a while and then flew away and did not come back.

Next Noah sent out a dove to see if the flood waters had gone down, but the dove could not find anywhere to land and, after a while, it flew back to the ark. Noah reached out his hand and lifted it in through the window.

He waited for another week; then he sent the dove out again.

"Adam and Eve in the Garden."

"The angels with the flaming sword."

On the evening of that day it came back and, in its beak, it held a fresh olive leaf. Now Noah knew that somewhere the waters had gone down far enough for the trees to be appearing again.

He waited one more week before he sent out the dove again. Out it flew, round and round, and out of sight. This time it did not return, and Noah knew that it must have found somewhere to settle among the trees.

A little time later, Noah was able to look out of the ark and to see that the ground was becoming drier. In time it became completely dry and the waters disappeared.

Then God said to Noah, "You may now leave the boat. Take your wife with you, and your sons and their wives, and all the birds and animals, so that they can settle on the earth and start having families again to replace all those that were drowned in the great flood."

So out came Noah and his family and all living creatures whom God had preserved during the great flood. The first thing Noah did was to take some stones and build an altar to God, to offer a sacrifice upon it and thank Him for keeping them safe.

God was pleased and said, "Never again will I destroy all living creatures as I have done this time. As long as there is a world, there will always be seed-time and harvest, cold and heat, summer and winter, day and night, and they shall not cease," and as He promised, all these things have gone on ever since.

As a sign of His promise to Noah, God said, "I shall put a rainbow in the cloud. Whenever the sky is cloudy and a rainbow appears, I will remember my promise to you and to all living creatures, that a flood will never again destroy all that live on the earth."

ABRAHAM AND ISAAC

IN the ancient city of Ur, in Babylonia, there lived a good man named Abram. One day, he and his wife Sarai set out from Ur to go to the land of Canaan.

Abram settled in the southern part of Canaan, and God said to him, "Look in all directions. This is the land which I am going to give you and your children and their children, and it will be yours for ever. You will have so many descendants that no one will be able to count them all."

Although Abram had no children at that time, he believed and trusted in God's word. He set up his camp near the sacred trees of Mamre at Hebron, and there he built an altar to the Lord.

One day the voice of God spoke to him and said, "I am the Almighty God. Obey me and always do what is right."

Abram bowed down and his face touched the ground. God repeated His promise that Abram would be the ancestor of many nations, and then He said, "Your name will no longer be Abram, but Abraham; no longer shall you call your wife Sarai; from now on her name is Sarah. I will bless her, and she will be the mother of many peoples, and there will be kings among her descendants."

Abraham must have found this news hard to believe, for both he and Sarah were very old.

One hot day Abraham was sitting by the door of his tent when he looked up and saw three strangers coming towards him. People were always very welcoming and polite to travellers in that country, so Abraham ran out, bowed to the men and said, "Sirs, please do not pass my door without stopping. Let me bring water to wash your feet and some food; it will help you on your journey. You have honoured me by coming here, so now let me serve you with the best that my house can provide."

"Thank you," said the newcomers. "We accept gladly."

So Abraham ran into the tent and said to his wife Sarah, "Quickly, let us prepare a meal for our visitors."

He took bread, cream, milk and some tender meat and set it before his guests.

Then the visitors asked him, "Where is your wife?"

"She is in the tent," answered Abraham.

"In the spring, she will have a son," said one of the men.

Sarah was just behind the tent entrance, and she laughed. "I am much too old to have a baby," she thought to herself, "and Abraham is too old to be a father."

"Why did Sarah laugh?" asked the strangers. "Is there anything which is too hard for the Lord to do?"

The strangers left and Abraham walked with them part of the way. By now he had realized that the men were messengers from God. He knew that if God had planned it, then Sarah would certainly have a son.

The promise which the strangers had brought to Abraham from God came true, and before long Sarah had a son, just as they had said. Abraham and Sarah were delighted, and they called the boy Isaac, which means "full of laughter". Perhaps this was

because they laughed with happiness when he was born, or it may
have been because they remembered Sarah laughing in the tent
when they first heard of their son yet to be born.

"God has brought me great joy and laughter," said Sarah.

Issac grew up to be a fine boy and his parents loved him very
much.

But when Isaac was still quite young, God put Abraham to the
test to see whether he really trusted Him.

He called to him one day, "Abraham! Take your son, your
only son, Isaac, whom you love so much, and set out for the land
of Moriah. I will show you a mountain there, and on it I want you
to offer your son as a sacrifice to Me."

Abraham must have wondered if he had heard God rightly. In
those days human sacrifices were not uncommon, and people
always offered to God the best that they had, but could God really
want Abraham to kill and offer his only son whom God Himself
had sent?

However, Abraham's trust in God was great. He believed that
God's commands must be obeyed, so he did not delay.

Early next morning he called Isaac and told him they were
going off into the mountains. He cut some wood for the sacrifice
and loaded it upon his donkey. Then, with Isaac and two of his
servants, he set out, walking with a sad and very heavy heart.

After three days' journeying, Abraham saw the mountain
ahead. He turned to the servants and said, "Stay here with the
donkey, while Isaac and I go over there to worship.

In saying this, he hoped that perhaps in some way God would
be able to save his son for him.

Abraham carried the knife and the coals for the fire, while

Isaac carried the wood. As they climbed the mountain, Isaac looked puzzled and said, "Father, we have the coals and the wood, but where is the lamb which we are going to sacrifice?"

All Abraham could reply was, "God Himself will provide one." With that Isaac had to be content, and they walked on.

When they arrived at the place of which God had told him, Abraham began to build an altar and to arrange the wood on it. Then he took Isaac and bound him and placed him on the altar on top of the wood. He raised the knife above his head.

At that moment the voice of an angel called out to him from heaven, "Abraham, Abraham!"

"Yes, here I am," answered Abraham.

"Do not lay your hand on the boy or do anything to hurt him. Now I know that you really trust God, because you have not kept back your only son from Him."

What a great relief Abraham felt! He looked round and there he saw a ram with its horns caught in a bush. God had sent it for him to sacrifice. He went over and freed it and offered it as a sacrifice in place of his son.

God was pleased with this great proof of Abraham's love and trust in Him.

Then the angel called to Abraham a second time and said, "God says, because you did this, and did not hold back your son, He will indeed bless you. You will have as many descendants as there are stars in the sky or grains of sand on the seashore, because you have obeyed His voice without question."

Abraham named the place of sacrifice Jehovah-Jireh, which means "The Lord will provide". Even today people say, "On the Lord's mountain He provides."

JOSEPH'S COAT

ISAAC, Abraham's son, married and had two sons of his own. One of these was named Jacob, and he had a very large family. He already had ten sons when an eleventh, named Joseph, was born.

Joseph became his father's favourite, and this made the other brothers very jealous. When Jacob gave Joseph a beautiful, long, multi-coloured robe, with sleeves, they were even more envious, for this was the kind of coat worn by persons of distinction.

Then the brothers hated Joseph so much that they could hardly speak a friendly word to him.

One night, when Joseph was still in his teens, he had a dream. Later he told his brothers about it.

"I dreamt we were all in the fields, tying up sheaves of wheat," he said, "and my sheaf stood upright while yours stood in a circle round mine and bowed down to it."

In those days people thought that dreams were a sign of what would happen in the future, so Joseph's brothers were naturally very angry at this and said, "Do you think you are going to be a king and reign over us then?"

Then Joseph had a second dream, which he told to his brothers and also to his father. "This time I saw the sun and the moon and eleven stars all bowing down to me," he said.

Jacob was not very pleased when he heard this, and he said,

"Do you mean that your mother, your brothers and I will all bow down to you?" but although he scolded Joseph, Jacob could not help thinking about the dream and wondering what it all meant.

Some time later, Joseph's brothers went to a place called Shechem to look for pasture for their sheep. When they had been gone some time, Jacob said to Joseph, "Will you go to Shechem and see if your brothers are safe and if the sheep are all right? Then come back here again and let me know.

Joseph agreed and off he went. However, when he arrived at Shechem he could not find his brothers, so he asked a man he met if he knew where they were. The man replied, "Yes, they've left here. I heard them say they were going to Dothan."

This was some four miles further on, but Joseph set off to find them nonetheless.

As he drew near to Dothan, his brothers saw him coming in the distance, and they began to plot against him. "Here comes the dreamer," they scoffed. "Let's kill him and throw his body into one of these pits. Then when we're asked, we can say that a wild animal has killed him. We'll see then what will become of his dreams!"

One of the brothers, named Reuben, was not very happy about this plan, and he tried to save Joseph. "Let us not kill him" he said, "but just throw him into the pit without hurting him—for after all, he is our brother." Reuben hoped he might be able to rescue Joseph later on and send him back to their father unhurt.

When Joseph came up, the brothers ripped off his splendid robe and threw him down into the pit. Then they sat down to have their meal.

Suddenly they heard a noise and looked up to see a procession of camels approaching. They belonged to a party of traders who were journeying to Egypt, and they were laden with all kinds of goods which the traders were taking to sell.

One of the brothers, Judah, had an idea. "What will we gain if we do kill Joseph and then have to cover up the murder?" he said. "Let's sell him to these traders instead; then we won't be hurting our own flesh and blood."

The brothers thought this a good idea and, when the traders came near, they hauled Joseph out of the pit and sold him to them for twenty pieces of silver.

Reuben hadn't been with them while this was happening; he had perhaps gone to tend to the sheep. When he came back and found Joseph gone, he was most upset. "What shall I do?" he cried. "The boy has gone!" But it was too late for him to do anything to save his brother.

Next the other brothers killed a goat and dipped Joseph's robe in its blood. Then they took the coat home and showed it to their father. "We found this," they exclaimed. "Does it belong to Joseph?"

"Yes, yes, it does!" cried the old man in horror. "Some wild animal must have killed him and torn him to pieces!"

Jacob wept and mourned for Joseph for a very long time. Although his family tried in every way to comfort him, he would not be consoled for the death of his favourite son. "I will still be mourning for Joseph when I die," he said.

Meanwhile, the traders and Joseph had arrived in Egypt, and there he was sold to a man named Potiphar who was one of the officers of the Pharaoh, the King of Egypt, and captain of the palace guard.

So Joseph lived in the house of his new Egyptian master and, because God was with him, he was successful in all that he did.

Potiphar made him his personal servant and put him in charge of his house and all that he owned. He found he could leave everything to Joseph and that Joseph was honest and did his work very well.

Potiphar's wife, however, was not so nice, and she told lies about Joseph to her husband. She said Joseph had behaved very wickedly towards her. This was completely untrue, but unfortunately Potiphar believed his wife and had Joseph thrown into prison.

Here the jailer soon realized that Joseph was indeed a trustworthy man, and so he put him in charge of the other prisoners. He also made him responsible for all the work that was done in the prison, and this relieved the jailer of many of his duties.

Some time later two other officials were put into the prison. One was Pharaoh's butler, or cup-bearer, and the other was his chief baker. Both had offended Pharaoh and they were due to spend a long time in jail.

One morning Joseph went to their cell and found them both looking very miserable. "What's the matter with you two?" he asked. "Why are you looking so worried?"

They answered, "We both had a dream last night and there is no one here who can tell us what the dreams mean."

"Only God knows the meaning of dreams," said Joseph. "But tell them to me and I will ask him to help us understand them."

So the butler said, "In my dream I saw a grapevine with three branches on it. The leaves came out, then the blossom and then the grapes ripened. I held Pharaoh's cup under the grapes and squeezed the juice into it and gave it to him."

"The three branches are three days", said Joseph, "and it means that in three days Pharaoh will set you free and restore you to your old position. Please remember me when you go out and ask Pharaoh if he will let me out of this prison—for I have done nothing wrong to deserve to be here."

Then the chief baker told his dream. "I was carrying three breadbaskets on my head," he began, "and in the top one were all kinds of baked food for Pharaoh, and the birds were eating them up."

Joseph told the baker that his dream had a sad meaning. "It means that in three days Pharaoh will have you hanged and the birds will eat your flesh." Three days later it was Pharaoh's birthday and he gave a party for all his officials. He released the butler and the baker, gave the butler his old job back, and had the chief baker hanged—just as Joseph had said.

However, when the butler was set free, he did not give Joseph another thought, and completely forgot to ask Pharaoh to have him set free.

Two years passed, and then something happened to remind the thoughtless butler that Joseph was still in prison.

Then Pharaoh himself had a dream. He dreamt he was standing by the River Nile when seven fat cows came out of the water and began to eat the grass. Then seven thin bony cows came up and stood by the fat cows on the riverbank; and the thin cows ate up the fat cows. And then Pharaoh woke up.

He soon fell aleep again and this time he had another dream. Now he saw seven fat, full ears of corn all growing on one stalk;

then seven more ears grew which were thin and damaged by the east wind. And the thin ears swallowed up the fat ones.

Pharaoh awoke feeling very worried. He knew it had only been a dream, but he was sure the dreams meant something. So he sent for all his magicians and courtiers and all his wise men and asked them, but none of them had any idea what the dreams meant.

Suddenly the butler remembered Joseph. At once he went to Pharaoh and said, "Two years ago you were angry with me and put me in prison along with the chief baker. While we were there, we both had a dream, and there was a young Hebrew man, also a prisoner, who was able to tell us the meaning of our dreams. And all he told us came true!"

"Send for him," commanded Pharaoh, and Joseph was quickly brought out of his dungeon. When he had washed and shaved himself and put on clean clothes, he went in to see Pharaoh. "I have had a dream," said Pharaoh, "and no one can explain it, but I have been told that when you hear a dream you can interpret it."

"No, your Majesty," said Joseph. "I can't, but God can. I can only tell you the interpretation which God gives me."

Then Pharaoh told his dreams to Joseph.

Joseph said, "The two dreams really mean the same thing, and through them God is telling you what is going to happen. The seven fat cows are seven years, and the seven full ears of corn are seven years; the seven thin cattle and the seven poor, empty ears are also seven years. What it means it that there will be seven years of plenty—good harvests and more than enough food for everyone. These will be followed by seven years of terrible famine and poor harvests—so bad that the seven good years will be entirely forgotten. The fact that you have had the dream twice means that the matter is fixed by God and that it won't be long before it happens.

"I think you should appoint a wise and careful man and put him in charge of the whole country. Then appoint overseers to take a fifth part of all the produce of the land during the seven good years. The officials can then store all this up. Thus it will be at hand when the famine comes, and so the people will not starve."

Pharaoh and his servants thought this was a very good idea. The only problem was where could they find a man wise, honest and clever enought to take charge of the whole plan. Then Pharaoh thought, "Who could be better than Joseph himself? The spirit of this God must be in him."

He said to Joseph, "Since your God has shown you all this, I will put you in charge of the country, and everyone must obey your orders. Only as regards the throne will I be greater than you. Your authority will be second only to mine. I will appoint you governor over all Egypt."

Then Pharaoh took a ring from his finger and put it on to Joseph's finger. He put fine linen robes on him and a gold chain round his neck; and he gave him his second-best chariot to ride in.

Joseph was thirty years old when he began his great task as governor of Egypt, and he travelled all over the country making provision for the famine which was ahead of them.

During the seven good years the land produced huge crops of corn, and Joseph had it collected and stored in the cities. There was so much corn that it was like the sands of the seashore and

Joseph soon stopped measuring how much there was. All the storehouses were packed full.

Then the seven years of plenty came to an end, and the seven years of famine started. There was famine in other countries as well, but because of Joseph's wise plan, there was food in Egypt. When the people felt hungry and went to Pharaoh, he told them, "Go to Joseph and do as he tells you." And Joseph opened the storehouses and sold the corn which he had stored.

People heard about it in other starving counries and they came from all over the world to buy some of Egypt's corn, because there was such a severe shortage everywhere else.

Joseph And His Brothers

The famine spread as far as Canaan, and when Jacob heard about the corn in Egypt, he said to his sons, "Why don't you do something about it? Don't just stand there looking at one another; go to Egypt and buy some grain to keep us from starving."

So the ten brothers set out on the long journey southwards to Egypt. There was now one more brother, who had been born after Joseph, and his name was Benjamin. Benjamin was now Jacob's favourite in place of Joseph, and his father would not allow Benjamin to go to Egypt with the others, because he was afraid that something might happen to the boy. So Benjamin remained at home.

When the ten brothers arrived in Egypt, they had to go first to Joseph like everyone else. He was busy organizing the buying and selling.

The brothers went and bowed low before him, and Joseph knew them immediately, but pretended not to; they did not recognize him in his Egyptian robes. Also he was talking in Egyptian and spoke to them through an interpreter. "Where do you come from?" he asked roughly.

"We've come from the land of Canaan to buy food," they replied.

"You are spies!" said Joseph. "You've come to find out where we are weak and open to attack."

"Oh no, sir," they said. "We have only come for food. We are all brothers, honest men—not spies, sir. We were twelve brothers in all, but one brother is dead and the youngest is at home."

Joseph wondered if they were sorry about the brother whom they thought was dead, and he decided to find out. "I think you are spies," he repeated, "but I will test you to find out. You will not leave here until I have seen this youngest brother you tell me about. One of you must go back and bring him, while the rest of you remain here under guard. This is how I will discover whether you are telling me the truth." And he put them all together in prison for three days. On the third day Joseph came to them and said, "I am a God-fearing man and I will let you go on one condition. That is that one of you stays here while the rest go back to take corn to your starving families. Then you must return, bringing back that youngest brother to me."

The brothers began preparing for their journey and talked among themselves as they did so. "It serves us right for what we did to Joseph," they said.

Reuben said, "I told you not to hurt him, didn't I? But you took no notice, and now look at us."

Joseph was secretly listening to all this, but because they thought he was an Egyptian, they did not know that he understood their words. It upset Joseph very much to hear them talking like this, and he left them because he was so overcome.

When he came back later, he chose Simeon, the second oldest brother, as the one to remain behind.

Then he gave orders for every brother's sack to be filled with grain, and he quietly added, "Put each man's money back in his sack, and give them all food for the journey home." The servants obeyed and brought the full sacks in to the brothers. Then the nine set off for Canaan.

When they came to rest for the night, one of them opened his sack to give food to his donkey. He was very surprised to find his money at the top of the bag, and it made all the brothers afraid.

When at last they reached home, they went and told Jacob all that had happened. As they emptied their sacks, each man found his money inside.

Jacob was very sad when they asked about taking Benjamin back. He said, "Joseph is gone, Simeon is gone, and now you want Benjamin!"

"I'll take care of him," said Reuben.

But Jacob would not be moved. "No," he said. "His brother Joseph is dead, and something might happen to Benjamin on the way. It would kill me."

However the famine in Canaan got worse, and the corn which the brothers had brought back was soon eaten. "You will have to go back and buy us a little more food," said Jacob to his sons.

"But we can't," said the fourth brother whose name was Judah. "The man said very sternly that he would not see us again unless we took Benjamin."

"Why did you bring about all this trouble by telling the man about Benjamin?" Jacob asked.

"The man asked us about ourselves; he thought we were spies. We had to answer his questions, and how were we to know what he would ask of us."

Judah said he would pledge his own life for the boy's. "Please

"Again the dove came back, but this time she had an olive leaf in her beak."

"Side by side Abraham and Isaac climbed the steep path that led
to the top of the mountain."

let us go at once, or we shall starve."

At last Jacob had to agree that Benjamin could go. "But take a present to the governor," he said, "and double the money that was returned before. Perhaps they made a mistake in giving the money back.

So the brothers and Benjamin set out for Egypt, and when they arrived they went into Joseph's presence. They were surprised when Joseph commanded that they should all go to his own house.

The brothers were afraid and thought they were to be punished because of the money which had been returned in their sacks. So they explained to Joseph's servant just what had happened.

"Don't worry," said the servant. "I received the payment all right. Your God must have put the money into your sacks." Then he brought Simeon to them, and took them all into the house.

When Joseph came in, they gave him their gifts and bowed low before him. "How are you?" asked Joseph. "And your father? Is he still alive and well."

Then he saw Benjamin. "So this is the youngest brother," he said. "God bless you, my son." Joseph felt as though he was about to break down, and had to leave the room hurriedly so that they would not see his tears. When he had washed his face, he came back and ordered the meal to be served. Joseph sat at a separate table, because Egyptians did not eat with Hebrews. The brothers sat in order of age at their table, from the oldest to the youngest. Food was served from Joseph's table, and the brothers noticed that Benjamin was given five times as much as anyone else.

After the meal, Joseph went to his servant and said, "Fill the men's sacks with food, as much as they are able to carry, and put their money in the tops of their sacks again. In the youngest boy's sack put my silver cup as well." The servant did so.

Early next morning, as soon as it was light, the brothers set off with their donkeys laden. They had not gone far when Joseph's servant, sent by Joseph, caught up with them and demanded, "Why have you stolen my master's silver cup?"

"We have done no such thing," protested the brothers in amazement. "Don't you remember that we brought back the money that we found in our sacks the last time—so why should we now steal from your master? If the cup is found in any of our sacks, that man shall die, and the rest of us will come back and be your master's slaves."

"All right," said the servant, "but only the one who has the cup shall be a slave; the rest of you can go free."

Feeling sure they had nothing to fear, the men allowed the servant to open their sacks, beginning with the eldest man.

Of course, the cup was found in Benjamin's sack. Shocked and unhappy, the brothers loaded their donkeys and returned to Joseph's house. Here Judah spoke up for them all. "Sir, what can we say? We must all be your slaves—not just Benjamin.

"No, no," said Joseph, "Only the one with the cup shall be my slave; the rest of you may go home."

"Please sir," said Judah, "let me speak, and don't be angry. We had to plead with our father for a long time before he would let Benjamin come, and now if we go back without him, our father will die of grief. He loves him particularly, because he has lost one son already. I made myself responsible for the boy, so let me stay here in his place."

Then Joseph could hold back no longer. He sent everyone out of the room except the brothers. Then he said, "Look, I am Joseph, the brother whom you sold into Egypt. But don't be upset or angry with yourselves because you sold me. You see, God sent me here to save people's lives. This is but the second year of famine, and there will be five more. Now I can rescue you and make sure that you do not starve."

Joseph went on, "Now hurry back to my father, and tell him that his son Joseph is alive and is ruler of all Egypt. Bring him back without delay, and you and all your families can come to live in the land of Goshen, where you will be near me. I don't want any of you to starve during the rest of the famine." Then he threw his arms round Benjamin and wept for joy, and he hugged his brothers too.

When the news reached the palace that the men from Canaan were Joseph's brothers, Pharaoh and his staff were delighted. Pharaoh ordered that when Jacob and the brothers and their families returned they should be given the best of everything in Egypt. The brothers were to take wagons and food for their journey back to Canaan. Joseph gave them all changes of clothing and sent presents back for Jacob.

"Joseph is alive!" they told Jacob when they got home, "and he is ruler over all Egypt!"

At first Jacob would not believe them—he was shocked. But when he saw the wagons that Joseph had sent to take him back to Egypt, he said, "Joseph is alive! I must see him before I die!"

So Jacob and his sons and their families packed their belongings and set off for the land of Egypt. On the way, at

Beersheba, Jacob stopped and offered sacrifices to God; and God said to him, "Don't be afraid to go to Egypt, for I will make you a great nation there. I will be with you, and I will bring your descendants back to this land."

When at last they reached the land of Goshen, Joseph came up in his chariot to meet his father. He threw his arms round his father's neck and wept for joy.

Then Joseph went to Pharaoh and told him that his father and brothers had arrived with their flocks and herds, and that they were now in Goshen. He took five of the brothers to Pharaoh.

"What is your occupation?" asked Pharaoh.

"We are shepherds, sir," replied the brothers.

Pharaoh turned to Joseph and said, "Let them settle in the land of Goshen, and if any are especially able men, put them in charge of my own cattle."

Then Joseph took Jacob in to Pharaoh, and Jacob blessed Pharaoh. Jacob and his family settled in Goshen, where they became rich and had many children. Eventually Jacob died there, but his body was taken back to Canaan to be buried.

THE BABY IN THE BULRUSHES

SOME years later, after Joseph had died, a new Pharaoh came to rule over Egypt. By this time Jacob's decendants, the Israelites, had been living in Egypt for many years, and there were now a great number of them.

The new Pharaoh knew nothing about Joseph and all that he had done to save the people from starvation, and he said, "These Israelites are getting so many that they might join up with our enemies. We must find a way to suppress them."

So the Egyptians put slave-drivers over the Israelites to make them work harder and harder, and they made them build store-cities for Pharaoh. The more cruelly they were treated, however, the more the Israelites seemed to increase in numbers. The Egyptians grew to fear them and made their lives miserable by being cruel and forcing them to work even more.

In the end Pharaoh issued an order that all baby boys born to the Israelites should be killed as soon as they were born. The nurses to whom this order was given refused to obey it, because they feared God, so finally Pharaoh made an order to all the people saying that every new baby boy born to the Israelites should be drowned in the River Nile, but that they could let the girls live.

Naturally the Hebrews were most unhappy about this law.

One family already had two children—a girl named Miriam and a boy named Aaron—and to them another baby boy was born. He was a fine baby, and the mother could not bear to see him drowned, so she managed to keep him hidden for three months.

As he grew bigger, the time came when she could hide him no longer, and so she and the family had to think of another plan. She made him a little basket from the bulrushes or reeds which grew at the side of the Nile and which were often used to make boats. Then she covered the basket with a tar-like substance to make it watertight. She put the baby into it and carried it down to the river. There she hid the basket among the reeds which were growing at the water's edge.

The baby's sister, Miriam, waited a little distance away to see what would happen to her baby brother.

Presently, Pharaoh's daughter came down to the river to bathe, and as she and her servants walked along the riverbank, she suddenly spotted the basket in the reeds. She sent one of her slave-girls to fetch it. The girl brought it and when it was opened the princess saw the baby boy. He began to cry and the princess felt sorry for him. "This is a Hebrew baby," she said.

Then his sister Miriam had an idea. She ran forward from where she had been hiding and said, "Shall I go and ask one of the Hebrew women to come and look after him for you?"

"Yes, please do so," answered Pharaoh's daughter, and clever Miriam hurried off and brought back her own mother.

"Take this baby and look after him for me," said the princess, "and I will pay you for doing so."

The baby's mother was delighted to have her own baby back again, although she may have realized that the princess would want to keep him in due course, when he was older. However, in the meantime, the mother gladly took back her own baby to nurse him in safety.

Later, when the boy was older, she took him again to Pharaoh's daughter, and the princess adopted him as her own son. "I drew him out of the water," she said, "and so I will call him 'Moses'. (The name 'Moses' sounded rather like the Hebrew word meaning 'to draw out'.)

So Moses grew up as a prince in Pharaoh's court, though he never forgot his own people.

When he was a young man, he went out to see how the Hebrews were living under the hard conditions of the Egyptians.

He was horrified when he happened to see an Egyptian kill one of the Hebrews. In his anger, Moses in his turn killed the Egyptian and buried his body in the sand. He thought no one had seen him, but that did not make his wrong-doing any better.

The next day, he went out again, and this time he saw two Hebrew men fighting. He went up to them and asked one of them, "Why are you fighting with one of your own countrymen?"

The man answered rudely, "Who made you a judge and ruler over us? Are you now going to kill me like you killed that Egyptian yesterday?"

Then Moses was afraid. "People know what I did," he thought to himself.

His wicked deed reached the ears of Pharaoh himself who thought that Moses deserved to be killed for what he had done. Moses was terrified and fled from the country, and went to live in the land of Midian. When he reached there, he sat down by a well, and at the same time the seven daughters of the priest of Midian, a man named Jethro, came down to draw water for their father's sheep and goats. Some shepherds tried to drive them away, but Moses went to their rescue and saw that they got the water for their animals.

When they reached home, their father asked how it was that they were back early that day. "An Egyptian helped us," they said. "He even drew the water for us."

"Why did you leave the man out there?" asked Jethro. "Go back and invite him to come and have a meal with us," he said hospitably.

So the girls went and brought Moses to their home. He agreed to live with them and helped to take care of Jethro's sheep and goats. After a time, he married one of the daughters whose name was Zipporah.

Many years later the Pharaoh of Egypt died, but the people of Israel were still suffering in their slavery, and they asked God to help them. God remembered the promises He had made to Abraham, to Isaac and to Jacob, and He promised He would send someone to deliver them from their bondage.

MOSES AND PHARAOH

ONE day, when Moses was looking after the flocks of his father-in-law, Jethro, he led them over the desert towards the west, until he came to the holy mountain named Sinai, or Horeb.

While he was there an angel appeared to him as a flame of fire coming from the middle of a bush. Although it was on fire, the bush itself did not seem to be burning up.

"This is strange," thought Moses. "I will go nearer and see why this bush is not burnt."

When he got closer, the voice of God called out,

"Moses! Moses!"

"Here I am," answered Moses.

"Do not come any nearer," said God. "Take off your shoes, for the place where you are standing is holy ground. I am the God of your ancestors, the God of Abraham, the God of Isaac, and the God of Jacob."

Moses hid his face, for he was afraid to look at God.

Then God said, "I know how cruelly My people are suffering in Egypt, and I have heard their prayers to be rescued from the Egyptians. I shall deliver them and bring them out of Egypt to a rich and fertile land. I shall send you to the King of Egypt so that you may rescue the Israelites from his country."

Moses was appalled at the thought of this tremendous task. He was sure he would not be able to do it, and he thought of one excuse after another, but God had the answer to each of them.

"I am nobody important," began Moses. "Who am I to go to Pharaoh? I am not up to such a job."

God answered, "But I will be with you."

"When you have brought the people out," said God, "you will worship Me on this mountain."

"How can I explain who You are?" asked Moses. "If I say, 'The God of your fathers sent me,' they will ask, 'What is His name?' What shall I say then?"

God replied, "I am who I am. Tell the people the one who is called 'I AM' has sent you, the God of Abraham, Isaac and Jacob. The people will listen to you. But when you ask Pharaoh to let the people go so that they may offer sacrifices to Me, I know he will not do so unless he is forced. I will use My powers and after that he will let you go."

But Moses still thought of the difficulties of this tremendous task. "What shall I do if the people don't believe me?" he asked. "Suppose they say You did not appear before me at all?"

God's answer to this was to give Moses three signs. First He asked Moses to throw the rod he was carrying on to the ground, and when he did so it became a snake. When God told him to pick it up by the tail, it became a staff again. "Do this to prove to the people that the Lord God has sent you," said God.

Next He told Moses to put his hand inside his robe, and when Moses did so his hand was suddenly diseased; but when he put it in and took it out a second time, it was normal and healthy again.

"If they are not convinced by that first miracle," said God, "then show them this second one. But if they don't believe even these two signs, take some water from the River Nile and pour it on the dry ground, and it will turn to blood."

Moses was still not happy. "Don't send me, Lord," he said. "I am no good at talking. I'm slow and have never been a good speaker."

God reminded Moses where all powers came from. "Who is it who gives a man his mouth? Who gives him sight?" He asked. "It is I, the Lord, and I will help you and tell you what to say."

"Lord God," implored Moses, "please send someone else."

God was not pleased that Moses did not trust Him enough to obey, but He replied, "Your brother Aaron speaks well. In fact, he is on his way to meet you now and will be glad to see you. You can go to Pharaoh together, and you can tell Aaron what to say. I will help you both, and he can be your spokesman. And take your staff with you, for with it you will be able to do great wonders."

So Moses went back to Jethro, his father-in-law, and said, "Let me go back to my people in Egypt and see if they are still alive."

Jethro understood and said, "Go in peace."

Before Moses left Midian, God reassured him by saying, "Go back to Egypt, for those who wanted to kill you are now dead."

Moses set out, and on the way he met his brother Aaron, as God had said. The brothers kissed one another, and Moses told Aaron all that God had said to him and all the signs and wonders that He had shown him.

Moses and Aaron went off to Egypt, and when they arrived they gathered together all the leaders of the Israelites. Aaron told them all that God had said to Moses, and Moses performed the miracles which God had shown him. The people believed him, and when they heard that God had seen their sufferings under the Egyptians, and that Moses and Aaron had been sent to deliver them, they bowed their heads and worshipped.

Together Moses and Aaron went to Pharaoh and said, "The Lord God of Israel says 'Let my people go, so that they can travel for three days into the desert and hold a festival in My honour.'" (The Israelites would have to leave Egypt to do this because their sacrifices would offend the Egyptians if they took place on Egyptian soil. The Egyptian religion was quite different from that of the Israelites.)

"Who is the 'Lord God'?" demanded Pharaoh haughtily. "Why should I do as he says? I don't know him and I won't let the Israelites go. You're making them neglect their duties. Get those slaves back to work! They are already more numerous than us Egyptians, and now you want to stop them working. No!"

He ordered the slave-drivers and foremen, "Stop giving the Israelites straw to make bricks. Make them find straw themselves—but they must still make the same number of bricks. They can't have enough work to do if they want me to let them go and make sacrifices to their God. If they work harder they won't have time to listen to such lies."

So the Israelites had to search all over the land for straw; if they failed to make the same number of bricks as before, the slave-drivers beat them. When the Israelites complained to Pharaoh, he said they were lazy and sent them back to work and the overseers beat them again.

The Israelite leaders blamed Moses and Aaron for going to Pharaoh at all. "You've only made matters worse," they complained. "You are not helping us at all!"

Moses prayed to God and said, "Why did You send me here? Pharaoh is treating the people even more cruelly since I came. It seems I have only made things worse for them."

"Tell the Israelites that I will rescue them from their slavery," said God, "and will bring them to the land which I promised to their ancestors." But the people were in such despair that they refused to listen to Moses and continued to grumble about their misfortunes.

Then God told Moses to go again to Pharaoh and to warn him that if he did not let the Israelites go, terrible things would happen in Egypt. "And if Pharaoh wants you to prove yourself," said God, "tell Aaron to thrown down his rod and it will become a snake."

Moses and Aaron did as God had said, and Aaron's rod did become a snake. Pharaoh called together all his magicians and wise men, and by their magic, they too made their sticks turn into snakes, but then Aaron's rod swallowed theirs up. Still Pharaoh refused to listen to Moses and Aaron and they were sent away.

Then God said to Moses, "Pharaoh is very stubborn. Go and meet him in the morning when he goes down to the river, and take your rod. Tell him that because he has not listened, he will know that I am the Lord by what he sees you do next. Then strike the surface of the river with your rod, and the water will turn into blood. No one will be able to drink from it. The same will happen to all rivers and pools and canals in Egypt and no one will have any water."

Moses and Aaron did as God commanded, and the Egyptians had to dig along the riverbanks for enough water to drink. But

Pharaoh paid no attenion and went back into his palace, saying it was all magic tricks.

A week passed and Moses went again to Pharaoh and said, "Let my people go. God says that if you do not, your country will be overrun with thousands of frogs."

Pharaoh refused, and God said to Moses, "Tell Aaron to hold his stick out over the waters, and frogs will come up and cover the land of Egypt."

Aaron did so, and frogs appeared, hopping everywhere. They went into the Palace, on to Pharaoh's bed, into all the people's houses, and even into the ovens and cooking pots. They jumped all over Pharaoh and his officials and on all the Egyptians. Pharaoh could bear it no longer, and he called Moses and Aaron and said, "Pray to your God to take these frogs away, and then I will let your people go." So Moses prayed to God, and the frogs died.

As soon as Pharaoh found that he was no more troubled by frogs, he changed his mind again and would not let the people go.

Then God sent a plague of gnats, which flew around and bit every man and animal. But still Pharaoh would not let the people go.

Next there came a plague of swarms of flies. The houses of the Egyptians were full of them, and the ground was covered with them, but there were no flies in the region of Goshen where the Israelites lived.

Pharaoh called for Moses and Aaron to come to him and said, "All right, you can offer sacrifices to your God, but you must do it here in this country where we can keep an eye on you."

"No, that wouldn't be right," said Moses, "because it would

offend the Egyptians. We must travel three days out of the desert."

"Provided you do not go very far," Pharaoh said. "And you must pray for me."

Moses asked God to take away the flies, and He did so. Once more Pharaoh changed his mind and would not let the people go.

Next there came a plague of cattle disease which killed the animals of the Egyptians, but not those of the Israelites—and still Pharaoh remained obstinate.

Then came a plague of boils, on both people and animals. Even so, Pharaoh would not listen to Moses and Aaron.

God told Moses that He would send a heavy hailstorm next day, such as had never been known before. He said that Pharaoh should order all people and animals to be under shelter, for those left outside, unprotected, would die. Some of Pharaoh's servants, who feared God, obeyed, but others took no notice and left their slaves and animals out in the open.

Then the hailstorm began, and there was thunder and lightning, far worse than Egypt had ever known; but in Goshen there was no storm at all. Any animal or person caught in the storm was killed and the crops damaged everywhere except where the Israelites lived.

Pharaoh was frightened and said to Moses, "I have sinned. Your God is right and I am wrong. We have had enough hail and thunder. I will let your people go." Moses went out and prayed to God, and the storm ceased. As soon as Pharaoh saw it, he became his old stubborn self again and refused to let the Israelites go.

Exasperated, Moses and Aaron went to him and asked, "How much longer will you defy God? If you keep on refusing, He will send a plague of locusts tomorrow, and they will eat up everything that the hail did not destroy."

"You may go," said Pharaoh, who had been persuaded by his officials to get rid of Moses or Egypt would be ruined. "But only the men," he added, "I won't let the women and children go. They must stay here."

Moses would have none of this and, as God had said, down came the clouds of locusts. The ground was black with them, and they ate everything until not a single green thing could be seen on any tree or plant. They ate all the harvest and the fodder for the animals too.

"I was wrong," cried Pharaoh. "Forgive me once more, and pray to your God to take away the locusts." God caused a strong wind to blow, and soon not one locust was left in Egypt. However the damage they had done was clear to everyone.

Yet again, Pharaoh had failed to learn his lesson, and he did not let the Israelites go. Then God sent a great darkness over Egypt for three days, so that the Egyptians could not see one another—although the Israelites still had light where they lived because God was protecting them.

"Go!" said Pharaoh to Moses. "And take your women and children too—but leave your animals behind."

But Moses refused to leave a single animal that belonged to his people and insisted that every donkey, ox, goat and sheep owned by the Childen of Israel should be free to leave Egypt with their owners.

"When the basket was brought, and the lid lifted, the baby woke
and wept, and the Princess took pity on him."

"The greatest gift of all was her little son, Samuel."

THE ESCAPE FROM EGYPT

PHARAOH had suffered nine plagues and yet had not learned to obey God. God told Moses that He would send one final punishment to the Egyptians and that then Pharaoh would certainly let the Israelites go.

So Moses went to Pharaoh with a final message from God and said, "The Lord says that at about midnight He will go through the land of Egypt, and every first-born son of every Egyptian will die, from your own son down to the son of the lowest maidservant, and the first-born of all the cattle will die too. Then," finished Moses angrily, "you will beg me to go, and I shall leave." Even this had no effect on Pharaoh, who did not change his mind.

And so it happened that, at midnight the first-born son of every family in Egypt died. Pharaoh and all his servants rose up during the night, and there was loud weeping in Egypt, because there was not one house in which the eldest son had not died. There was great sorrow throughout Egypt. The animals died also, just as Moses had told Pharaoh they would, but not one Israelite died or any animal that belonged to an Israelite.

Pharaoh summoned Moses and Aaron that same night and said, "Get out! You and all the people of Israel. Go and worship your God, and take your flocks and herds too. And pray for a

55

blessing for me also."

The Egyptian people were anxious to see the Israelites go as well. "Hurry up and leave our country," they said, "otherwise we shall all be dead." And they gave the Israelites gold and silver and clothing and anything else which they asked for.

The Israelites packed up their belongings and hurriedly left the land of Egypt—so quickly that they did not have time to get food ready or prepare leavened bread.

Happily they set out on foot, a great company of them, free at last from the bondage of Pharaoh! There were about 600,000 men, women and children, and all their sheep and goats and cattle went with them. There were also a number of other races and Egyptians with them, who had married Israelites or were slaves to them for the Israelites had slaves of their own.

They had been in the land of Egypt for 430 years, and so none of them knew what it was like to be free.

The way from Egypt to Canaan was north east, but it is not absolutely certain which route the Israelites took. It is thought that they did not take the coast road, because there they would have met with Philistine forces, and they were not ready for such an encounter. Instead they began in a generally southerly direction, and at some point crossed the Red Sea, or 'sea of reeds', which may then have extended further north than it does now.

The long procession left Egypt to head for he promised land of which God had told their ancestors and God Himself went in front to show them the way. He appeared as a pillar of cloud during the day and as a pillar of fire during the night; thus they had light and so could travel both night and day.

They had not been long on the way when Pharaoh and some of his officials had second thoughts about letting them go. "Who will now do the work which those slaves did?" they asked. "Why ever did we let them escape like that?" So Pharaoh decided they must try and bring the Israelites back. He got ready his war chariot and his army and 600 of the best and fastest chariots in the land, and they all chased off after the Israelites.

When the Israelites saw them coming, they were terrified. They were hemmed in by sea and mountains, with the Red Sea in front of them and Pharaoh and his chariots behind them, and they cried out in terror to Moses. "Did you have to bring us here to die? Aren't there any graves in Egypt? Look what you've done now! We'd have been better staying as slaves to the Egyptians than dying out here in the wilderness."

"Don't be afraid," said Moses. "Just stand firm and you will see what God will do to save you. He will fight for you. There is no need for you to do anything."

Moses knew that the right thing to do was to trust God, and he wanted the people of Israel to trust Him too.

God said to Moses, "Why do you cry out to Me? Tell the people to move forward. Then lift up your rod and hold it over the water; the sea will divide and you may all walk through on dry ground." Moses agreed to do so.

Then the pillar of cloud moved back until it was between the Israelites and the Egyptians, and so the night passed without the two forces coming near to one another.

The next day Moses held out his rod over the water, and God sent a strong east wind which blew all night and drove the waters back so that they were divided. Then the people were able to walk through on dry land, with water on both sides of them.

Pharaoh's army saw their chance and galloped into the water after them, with all their horses, chariots and horsemen. But their chariots were so heavy that they began to sink in the soft ground, and their wheels became clogged with mud so that they found it difficult to move. The Egyptians said to one another, "Let's go back out of here, for God is fighting on the side of the Israelites and is against us, the Egyptians."

"Hold out your hand over the sea," said God to Moses, "and the waters will come back over the Egyptians and their chariots and horses." Moses did so, and by next morning the sea was flowing normally and not one of the Egyptians had reached the other side.

From the far shore the Israelites could see how God had saved them yet again from the Egyptians. There was great rejoicing and the people began to sing in praise of God. Miriam, Moses and Aaron's sister, and all the other women took up tambourines and danced and sang in praise of God who had delivered them from their enemies.

THE TEN COMMANDMENTS

UNDER God's guidance, Moses led the people on, away from the Red Sea, and across a great stretch of desert called the Wilderness of Shur. The land was hot, dry and barren, full of sand dunes, scrubland and rocks, and with hardly any water. When they had been travelling for three days, the Israelites became very thirsty and were delighted when they found water at a place called Marah. When they came to drink it, however, they found it very bitter. "What are we going to drink?" they grumbled to Moses.

Moses prayed to God, and God showed him a tree whose bark and leaves are able to sweeten bitter water. Moses threw some of this into the water, and the water became fit to drink.

From Marah, the Israelites moved on to Elim, where they found twelve springs of water and seventy palm trees, and here they were able to camp and rest for a while. They could not stay long, however, for they had to continue their journey, and soon they were grumbling again.

"We're hungry," the people complained. "At least we had food in Egypt, but now you have brought us out here we shall all starve to death."

God told Moses, "I shall send food for you. Each day the people must go out and gather enough for that one day. On the sixth day of the week, they are to gather twice as much as usual."

That evening a large flock of little brown birds called quail flew into the Israelites' camp; and the people found that their flesh was good to eat.

In the morning, when the dew had gone, the ground was covered with a thin flaky substance, like small white seeds, and as delicate as hoar-frost.

"*Manna?*"asked the Israelites, which means, "What is it?", and so "manna" became its name

Moses said, "This is the food which God has provided. You are each to gather as much as you need for the day, but no extra.

The Israelites began gathering, and some gathered more and some less; but it made no difference. Those who had gathered more found that they did not have too much, and those who had gathered little found that there was enough for their needs. Any which was left on the ground melted in the heat of the sun by midday. In spite of Moses's order, some people tried to save some for the next day, but found that it rotted overnight.

Only on the sixth day of the week could they gather twice as much as usual and then it did not go bad; for the seventh day, the Sabbath, was their day of rest, and they were not to gather food on that day. Though some people did go out looking for the manna on the seventh day, there was none to be found. God said to Moses, "How much longer will the people disobey My commands? Remember that I gave you a day of rest, and that is why I will always provide twice the amount of food on the sixth day. On the seventh day they must stay at home."

God continued to provide manna for the Israelites for the whole of the next forty years until they reached the land of Canaan.

Food was one thing difficult to find in the desert, but, as the Israelites had already discovered, water was another. As they moved on, they again grumbled to Moses that they were thirsty. "Why do you keep complaining like this?" asked Moses.

Once again the people said, "Why did you bring us out of Egypt to this miserable place? Must we all die of thirst?" And they grew very angry.

"What can I do with them?" Moses asked God.

"Take some of the leaders and go on ahead of the people," said God. "Carry your rod. I will stand before you on a rock on Mount Sinai. Speak to the rock and water will flow out from it."

Moses went as the Lord had said, but he was so angry with the people that instead of just speaking to the rock, as he had been told, he struck it with his staff. A stream of water flowed out, just the same, and the people and animals were able to quench their thirst. But Moses had not obeyed God and so God told him that he would not be the one to lead the people into the promised land.

By now the Israelites had crossed much desert land and had come to the foot of Mount Sinai. From the mountain God called Moses and said, "Tell the people that I have said these words, 'You saw what happened to the Egyptians and how I have brought you safely to this place. Now if you will obey Me and keep My covenant, you will be My chosen people, dedicated to Me alone."

When the people heard this they replied, "We will do all that the Lord has said."

God then told Moses that the people were to make themselves ready for worship and were to put on clean clothes, for He

Himself would come down on Mount Sinai. Moses was to put a boundary round the mountain, and the people were not to cross it, or even go near it until they heard a trumpet sounding a long blast.

The people made themselves ready as instructed. On the third day there was thunder and lightning and thick cloud on the mountain, which indicated God's power and presence, and a loud blast was heard on a trumpet. All the people trembled with fear. Moses led them to the foot of the mountain, which was wrapped in fire and smoke and shook as if there was an earthquake.

Then God called to Moses alone to go to the top of the mountain; and Moses went up and was lost to view in the cloud. He remained up there for forty days.

While Moses was on the mountain, God gave him the laws by which the Israelites were to live. Among these laws were those which are known as the Ten Commandments, which were written on two tablets of stone by God Himself.

These are the Ten Commandments.

1 *You shall have no other gods before me.*
2 *You shall not make for yourself a graven image, or any likeness of anything that is in heaven above, or that is in the earth beneath or that is in the water under the earth; you shall not bow down to it or serve it.*
3 *You shall not take the name of the Lord your God in vain.*
4 *Remember the sabbath day, to keep it holy. Six days you shall labour, and do all your work; but the seventh day is a day dedicated to the Lord your God; on it no one shall do any work. For in six days the Lord made heaven and earth, the sea, and all*

that is in them, and rested on the seventh day; therefore He blessed the sabbath day and made it holy.

5 *Honour your father and your mother.*

6 *You shall not kill.*

7 *You shall not commit adultery.*

8 *You shall not steal.*

9 *You shall not bear false witness (tell lies) against your neighbour.*

10 *You shall not covet (long to possess) your neighbour's house or wife, or his manservant, or his maidservant, or his ox, or his ass, or anything that belongs to your neighbour.*

Moses was away for such a long time that the people grew tired of waiting. They gathered around his brother Aaron and said, "We don't know what has become of Moses, and we can't wait any longer. Let us make a god of our own."

Aaron, on this occasion, was not firm, and he said to the people. "Take off the gold earrings which you are wearing and give them to me."

They did so, and Aaron took the huge pile of earrings, melted them down, and shaped the gold into a golden calf. Forgetting all about the one true God, the people looked at the golden calf and said, "This is the god who led us out of Egypt."

Aaron built an altar before it, and declared that the next day was to be a festival to the Lord. Perhaps he, too, thought it represented the true God, though he should have known better.

Early on the next day, the people brought animals for offerings and they had a great feast.

High up on the mountain God said to Moses, "You must go down to the people, for they have already forgotten the way I commanded them, and they have made a calf of melted gold and are worshipping that. I am very angry with them."

So Moses set off back down the mountain, carrying the two stone tablets on which God had written the Ten Commandments. As he was getting near the foot of the mountain, he could hear shouting and noise coming from the people. When he came close enough he saw that they were dancing round the golden calf, and he was so furious that he threw down the tablets and they broke.

He seized the golden calf, melted it and ground what remained to powder. Then he scattered the powder upon the water and made the Israelites drink it as a symbol of their shame and regret.

The next day he went back to God and asked His forgiveness for the sin which the people had committed in worshipping the golden calf. At God's command, he also cut two more tablets of stone, and God gave him the laws again. As a token that they were forgiven, God renewed His promise, or covenant, to the people.

SAMUEL

THE story of how Moses led the Children of Israel out of Egypt is a long one, and is full of adventures. Even after the people had reached the land of their ancestors, they could not live in peace, for they had to fight to gain control of their country. Gradually, they managed to spread out over the land of Canaan, building homes and farms for themselves. Even so, their neighbours, especially a group of people called the Philistines, were always a problem. But God was with the people, and in order to help them, He sent Samuel. This is his story.

In Ramah, not far from Jerusalem, there lived a man named Elkanah. He had two wives, which was not uncommon in those days; one, named Peninnah, had children, but the other, named Hannah, had none.

Each year the whole family went up to Shiloh, where the Tabernacle was placed, to offer sacrifices; and each year Hannah felt sadder and sadder because she had no children to take with her. Penninah was not kind about it and used to tease her, so much so that Hannah often wept.

One year Hannah went unhappily into the house of the Lord of Shiloh, and prayed to God that He would send her a son, "I will dedicate him to You for his whole life," she said.

Eli, the old priest there, saw her distress and her lips moving, and thought at first that she must be drunk. But when he went up to her, Hannah told him of her trouble. "Go in peace," said Eli, "and may God answer your prayer."

God did. In due course Hannah had a fine baby boy, whom she named Samuel. As soon as he was old enough, Hannah fulfilled her promise and took him to the house of the Lord at Shiloh. "Do you remember me?" she asked Eli. "This is the child whom God sent to me in answer to my prayer. I have brought him here to dedicate him to the Lord."

So Samuel became a helper to old Eli, and Eli was very glad of his aid. He did have two sons of his own, but they were worthless and dishonest men who had no respect for God or His house.

Every year Hannah came and saw Samuel, and brought him a new robe; and God blessed her further by sending her three more sons and two daughters.

Time passed and Eli grew old and was almost blind. He slept in his own room in the Lord's house, while Samuel slept near the Covenant Box in the sanctuary.

One night, after Samuel had fallen asleep, he was suddenly awakened by a voice calling, "Samuel! Samuel!"

Thinking it was Eli, Samuel got up and ran to the old man. "Here I am," he said. "You called me."

"No," said Eli, "I did not call. Go back to bed."

Samuel obeyed, but before long he heard the voice again, "Samuel!"

Again he got up and ran to Eli, but Eli said, "I did not call, my son; go and lie down again."

Samuel did so, and the voice called him a third time, and Samuel, feeling puzzled, went again to Eli. By now, Eli had begun to understand that it was the voice of God who was calling Samuel. So he said to the boy, "Go back and if you hear the voice again, say, "Speak, Lord, for your servant is listening'."

Samuel returned to bed, and sure enough, the voice called again, "Samuel! Samuel!", and Samuel replied as Eli had told him. Then God gave Samuel a sad message. He told him that Eli's family would have to suffer punishment because of the wickedness of Eli's sons.

Samuel stayed in bed until morning, when he got up and opened the doors of the house of the Lord. At first he was afraid to tell Eli of God's message, but Eli asked him, and Samuel told him everything.

Eli looked sad, but said, "He is the Lord, He will do what He knows is best."

Samuel grew up to be a prophet, a fine man who preached God's word. Not everyone listened, however; there were still many who worshipped idols and refused to obey God's laws.

One day, when Samuel was an old man, the people went to him and asked him to appoint a king over them. Samuel prayed to God for help.

Now, there lived a rich man named Kish, who was of the tribe of Benjamin, and he had a handsome son named Saul. Saul was a head taller than most other people, and so he was easily noticed in a crowd. It so happened that Kish's donkeys had wandered away and were lost; so Kish said to Saul, "Take one of the servants and go and look for those donkeys."

Saul and the servant set off, and walked for about three days, but still they did not find the animals. Finally Saul said, "Let's go back, or my father will worry about us, as well as the donkeys."

"Just a moment," said the servant. "There is a holy man living in this area; let us just see if he can help us." So they set off for the town in which the holy man lived.

The holy man was none other than Samuel and, on the day before, God had told him that he would send a man whom Samuel was to anoint King of Israel. When Samuel saw Saul coming towards him, God said to him, "This is the man."

Saul went up to Samuel and asked where the holy man lived. "I am he," said Samuel. "Come and eat with me; and don't worry about the donkeys, for they have been found. The man the people of Israel have wanted so much is you."

"But I belong to the smallest tribe in Israel—the tribe of Benjamin," said Saul, "and my family is not very important."

Samuel took Saul and his servant inside, where there were about thirty people, and they all sat down to a meal. After this Saul was given a bed for the night—up on the roof, where it was cooler. He felt very puzzled.

Next morning, Saul and his servant were up early, ready to be on their way; Samuel went to the edge of the town with them. There he said, "Tell your servant to go on ahead."

When the servant had gone, Samuel took a jar of oil and poured it on Saul's head saying, "The Lord has anointed you to be ruler of his people Israel." And he gave him certain signs to prove it was true.

King Saul began his reign well, and although there were some people who did not at first respect him, when they found he was a good leader, they began to obey him. Later on, however, he became self-willed and arrogant, and did not live up to the high hopes which people had of him.

Before long, the Philistines were again assembling to fight the Israelites. They mustered a huge army of war chariots and horsemen and countless soldiers, and many of the Israelites were terrified and deserted Saul.

Samuel had told Saul to wait seven days for him to come, but Saul thought he knew better and when he saw the people scattering from him, he began to offer a sacrifice without waiting for Samuel. As soon as he had finished, Samuel arrived. He was displeased and told Saul that this disobedience would cost him his kingship, and that God would find another man to become ruler in his place.

The battles against the Philistines went on, but Saul did not continue to be a strong king, for he had disobeyed God's commands.

Then God said to Samuel, "Take some oil and go to Bethlehem, to a man whose name is Jesse, for I have chosen one of his sons to be the next king."

Samuel was rather worried about this. "How can I go?" he asked. "If Saul hears about it he will kill me."

"Take a calf with you," said God, "and go there to offer sacrifice. Then I will show you what to do."

Samuel did as God had instructed, and when the elders of the town came out to meet him, he invited them to join in the sacrifice.

When he saw Jesse and his family, he particularly noticed his son Eliab, and thought to himself, "Surely this is the man whom the Lord has chosen."

But God said to Samuel, "Do not just look at his appearance or his height, because he is not the man. I, the Lord, do not see as men see. Men look at the outward appearance, but I look at a man's heart."

Then Jesse brought out his son Abinadab, but Samuel knew that he was not the chosen one either.

Seven of Jesse's sons came out to Samuel, but the Lord did not choose any of them. "Are all your sons here?" asked Samuel. "Are there no more?"

"There is only the youngest," said Jesse, "but he is out looking after the sheep."

"Send and fetch him," said Samuel, "for we won't start the sacrifice until he comes."

So Jesse's youngest son, David, was brought in. He was a handsome youth, with beautiful eyes; and God said to Samuel, "This is the one I have chosen; anoint him."

Samuel took the horn of oil and anointed David in front of his brothers who may have thought that this meant David would become Samuel's follower, and in time became a prophet like himself. God's spirit came to David on that day, and Samuel then returned to Ramah.

Meanwhile, evil forces had taken charge of Saul, who often became depressed and even violent. His servants thought it might help if he could be soothed with music, so they said, "Give us the order, sir, and we will find someone who can play the harp. Then when the evil spirit torments you, the musician can play his harp and you will be all right again." Saul agreed, and asked for a musician to be brought to court.

One of the servants had an idea. "There is a man named Jesse in Bethlehem," he said, "and he has a son who is a good musician. He is also brave and handsome."

"All through the royal rooms the sweet music floated, and Saul was
refreshed and made well."

"God sent Elijah bread and meat by ravens."

"Go and bring him," Saul ordered.

Messengers went to Jesse, and Jesse sent David to the king's court, with gifts of a young goat, a donkey laden with bread, and a leather skin full of wine.

Saul liked David, and sent a message to Jesse to say how pleased he was with his son. From then on, whenever Saul felt tormented by the evil feelings, David was sent for and would bring his harp and play it; and Saul would soon feel better again.

THE STORY OF DAVID

THE fierce battles with the Philistines continued, and at last the Israelite and Philistine armies found themselves facing one another across the mountains with the Valley of Elah between them.

One morning there came out from the Philistine camp two men. The first was a soldier carrying a shield, but it was the man behind him who made the Israelites gasp with horror. He was an enormous giant of a man, nearly 10 feet tall, and dressed in a bronze helmet and heavy bronze armour on his legs, and he carried a huge bronze javelin. His great thick spear had a wicked-looking head of iron on it. The name of this giant was Goliath, and the Israelites trembled at the sight of him.

He stood and glared across at the ranks of the Israelites; then he roared across to them in a terrible voice, "What do you think you are all doing there lining up for battle? I am a Philistine and you are Saul's slaves. Choose one of your number and send him to fight me! If he can kill me, then we will be your slaves; but if I win, then you shall be our slaves and serve us. I dare you to send somebody to do battle with me!"

The Israelites were terrified and did not dare send anybody. They were pretty sure who would win when they looked at Goliath! No one in their army could have a hope of beating him;

so nobody went out to meet him.

Goliath continued to roar his challenge at them. Every morning and every evening for the next forty days he bellowed across at the Israelites. Saul and his army were dismayed and felt more and more discouraged.

Now Jesse was too old to go and fight in Saul's army, but his three eldest sons had gone—Eliab, Abinadab and the third son whose name was Shammah. David was still taking care of his father's sheep.

One day Jesse said to David, "Go to your brothers in the army, and take them some food—some roasted grain and loaves of bread. See how they are getting on, and bring back something to prove to me that they are well. Take ten cheeses for their commanding officer also."

Early next morning David got up, ready for his journey. He left someone else in charge of the sheep and set off with the food which his father had given him.

When he reached the camp, both armies were just preparing for battle. David handed the food to the officer in charge of supplies, and ran in among the soldiers to find his brothers. As he was chatting to them, Goliath came out for his twice-daily challenge to the Israelite, clanking his armour and roaring defiance. The Israelite soldiers were becoming worn down by this performance, and they ran away, trembling.

David asked the soldiers near him what it was all about and they said, "King Saul has promised a big reward to anyone who kills this giant, and he will also give him his daughter to marry and free him of taxes."

"Who is this heathen Philistine to dare to defy the army of the living God?" said David scornfully.

Some of the soldiers told Saul what David had said, and the king sent for him. "Your majesty," said David. "I'll volunteer to go and fight this giant. No one should feel afraid of him."

"No, no," said King Saul. "You are only a boy. He's been a fighting soldier all his life."

"But sir," said David, "I look after my father's sheep, and if a bear or a lion comes to seize a lamb, I rescue the lamb, and kill the bear or lion. I've killed many such, and I'll kill this Philistine. The Lord has saved me from lions and bears, and He will save me from this Philistine."

Saul was impressed. "All right," he said, "you can go and try. No one else has offered. You may wear my helmet and my armour. And God be with you."

When David was dressed in Saul's armour, he found he could not walk in it; it was so heavy, and he was not used to wearing armour. So he took it all off and went to meet Goliath with only his stick and his sling. On the way he piced up five smooth stones from the stream and put them in his shepherd's bag.

As soon as Goliath saw who was coming to fight him, he laughed with scorn. "What's the stick for, boy?" he shouted. "Do you think that I am a dog?"

David replied, "You are coming to me with might—your sword and spear and javelin. But I come to you in the name of the living God, the God of Israel whom you have defied. I will defeat you, and the whole world will know that Israel has the true God."

With that, he ran towards Goliath, taking one of the stones from his bag. He aimed it straight at Goliath's forehead, and it struck the giant who fell on his face on the ground. David ran over and, taking Goliath's own sword from its sheath, he killed the giant.

When the Philistines saw what had happened to their champion, they turned and fled, hotly pursued by the Israelites who won a great victory.

After this great victory, David was taken into the presence of King Saul. While he was at the court, he met Saul's son, Jonathan, and came to like him very much. A firm bond grew up between them and they swore eternal friendship. Saul treated David almost like another son, and David did so well in all the missions that he was given that Saul made him a commander in the army, and everyone was delighted with the news as David was very popular.

When the army returned home after their victory over the Philistines, the people danced and sang for joy. "Saul has slain his thousands, but David his tens of thousands," they cried. Now Saul did not like to hear this and he began to grow jealous of David. He even began to be afraid of his success. But the people all loved David because he was such a great leader.

In due time, David married Saul's daughter, Michal; but Saul grew more and more moody and had many attacks of bitter jealousy against David for no reason at all.

One day, Jonathan found out that Saul was actually plotting to kill David, so he warned David to go and hide. "I will talk to my father, and if I find out anything, I will tell you," he said to David. Then he went to his father, and reminded him of all the great things David had done. Saul listened and understood, and decided that David should not be killed. So David came out of hiding and served the king once more.

It was not for long, however; another time, Saul's jealous mood returned, and he hurled a spear at David as he was playing the harp. David managed to dodge it and so was not hurt. That night Saul sent some men to David's house to kill him; but David's wife, Michal, heard of it, and let David down from a window so that he escaped. Then she took the figure of an idol from the house and put it in the bed, so that when the soldiers came looking for David, they were tricked and David was able to make his escape in the midst of the confusion.

Naturally, David grew very worried about these attempts on his life, and he asked Jonathan one day, "What have I done? What crime have I committed that makes your father want to kill me? I have always been his loyal servant."

Jonathan wanted to do all he could to help his friend and thought that his father would tell him what he was about to do; but David thought that as Saul knew he and Jonathan were friends, he would not tell Jonathan anything about his plots against David.

The next day was the Feast of the New Moon, and David was supposed to dine with the king. He decided not to go, but to hide in the fields instead. He said to Jonathan, "If your father notices that I am not there, tell him that I have gone to Bethlehem to attend the yearly sacrifice there for all the family. If he says 'All right', then I'll be safe. If, however, he is angry, then you will know that he plans some evil against me."

Jonathan agreed to let David know what happened. Saul did notice David's absence and asked Jonathan about it. When Jonathan said David had gone to Bethlehem, Saul flew into a rage and said, "Bring him here immediately, for he must die!"

"But why?" asked Jonathan reasonably. "What wrong has he done?"

For an answer Saul angrily threw his spear at Jonathan, but did not hurt him.

Jonathan was upset and ashamed of his father's evil mood, and the next day he went out into the fields and let David know that he must flee and escape Saul's anger. "God be with you," said Jonathan to David. "The Lord God will be with us and our descendants for ever."

For a long time there was war between Saul and his men and David and his followers. Yet on two occasions when he had a chance to kill Saul, David would not do so; no doubt he remembered that Saul had once treated him like a son, and, moreover, had he not been anointed king by Samuel, acting on God's instructions?

In the end, King Saul was killed in a battle against the Philistines. Three of his sons were killed in the same battle, and one of them was Jonathan, David's beloved friend.

After this, David was made king, and he reigned for forty years, well and wisely.

ELIJAH

WHEN David died, his son Solomon became King. But after Solomon's death, civil war broke out in Israel, and the country became divided into two kingdoms. The tribes of Judah and Benjamin formed the Kingdom of Judah in the south, and the remaining ten tribes formed the Kingdom of Israel in the north. The latter had a succession of kings, but none was very good; these included one of the worst kings ever—Ahab of Israel. He had a wife named Jezebel who was, if anything, worse than he was. Both of them worshipped the Philistine god, Baal.

Now, as often happened, God chose someone to pass on His message. This was a prophet called Elijah, who was not afraid of speaking out for God. He went to Ahab and said there would be no more rain until God (not Baal) said so. God had decided to teach Ahab and his followers that only He had power over sun and rain.

Then God told Elijah to go to the brook called Cherith, where ravens would bring him food each day and he would be able to drink from the stream. This Elijah did, but because there was no rain, after a while the brook dried up.

Elijah then went to stay with a widow and her young son. They gave him food—though they had little enough for themselves. But, because God was looking after them, the widow's supply of food, small though it was, never ran out in all the time Elijah was with her.

No rain fell upon the land for three years, and the drought and the famine grew very severe. In the third year God said to Elijah, "Go to Ahab, and I will send rain."

About this time Ahab was talking to a man named Obadiah, who was in charge of the palace household. Obadiah was a good man who believed in God, and had even rescued some of God's prophets from the wicked Queen Jezebel when she was about to kill them.

Ahab said to Obadiah, "Go out and see if you can find enough grass anywhere to keep the animals alive."

Obadiah set off, and on his way whom should he meet but the prophet Elijah coming to see Ahab. "Go and tell your master that I am here," said Elijah.

Obadiah was rather fearful. "The king has been looking for you in every country," he said, "and if I tell him you are here, and you have moved on by the time he gets to you, then he will surely kill me."

"Go and tell him," said Elijah, "I will see him today."

So Obadiah went and told Ahab, and Ahab set off to meet Elijah. When he saw the prophet he said, "There you are—the man who is causing all this trouble in Israel!"

"I'm not causing any trouble," said Elijah; "it is you and your people who have disobeyed God's commands and are worshipping idols."

Ahab could not deny this and he did not attempt to.

Elijah went on, "Order all the people of Israel to come to Mount Carmel. Bring along the 450 prophets of Baal and the 400 prophets of Asherah whom Queen Jezebel supports."

Ahab had little choice. He thought it possible that Elijah's God would send rain, so he gathered the people together.

Elijah looked around at the crowd gathered upon Mount Carmel. "How long are you going to dither between two ways?" he thundered. "If the Lord is God, follow Him, but if Baal is god, follow him."

There was silence. The people did not know what to say.

"I am the only prophet of the Lord here," said Elijah, "but there are 450 prophets of Baal. Now, bring two bulls for a sacrifice. Let us each take one and put it on the wood, but do not light the fire. Then we shall each pray to our god to send fire, and the one who answers, then he is God."

The people agreed, and Elijah let the prophets of Baal go first as there were so many of them. They took the bull and prepared it and put it on the wood. Then they cried to Baal from morning until noon, calling, "O Baal, answer us!" They shouted and danced around, but there was no reply.

"Shout a bit louder," teased Elijah. "Perhaps your god has gone on a journey, or perhaps he is asleep. You must waken him." So the prophets of Baal cried louder and danced about in a frenzy, cutting themselves with their knives and daggers, which was one of their customs. But still there was no answering voice, and no fire.

When they had all worn themselves out, Elijah said, "Now it is my turn." The people gathered round him and watched while he repaired the altar which had been torn down. He took twelve stones, one for each of the twelve tribes of Israel, and built it up, and then dug a trench around it. He put the wood on the altar, and the bull upon the wood. Then he ordered water to be poured over the whole thing, not once, but three times, until the whole trench was full of water, and the wood was soaking wet.

Then he prayed, "O Lord God, show that You are the true God, so that these people will know You want to bring them back to the true faith."

Immediately fire came down from heaven, and burnt up the bull and the wood and the stones and the dust; it even dried up the water that was in the trench. When the people saw this, they were overawed and fell down on their faces, crying, "The Lord, He is God; the Lord, He is God."

"Seize the prophets of Baal," commanded Elijah. "Let none of them escape! They have led you wrongly." The prophets were seized and put to death, by which act the people really proved that they knew they had a new God.

Then Elijah turned to Ahab and said, "Go and eat, for I hear that rain is coming." While Ahab was going, Elijah and his servant climbed up to the top of Mount Carmel. "Go and look towards the sea," said Elijah, and the servant went.

"I see nothing," he said

"Go again", said Elijah, "seven times."

At the seventh time, the servant returned and said, "I saw a cloud, no bigger than a man's hand, rising up out of the sea."

"Then go and tell King Ahab to get into his chariot and go home before the rain stops him," said Elijah.

Soon the sky was covered with dark clouds and the wind began to blow, and great heavy raindrops started to fall. Elijah fastened his robes about him, and ran ahead of Ahab's chariot, all the way back to Jezreel where Ahab's palace was.

THE NEW

TESTAMENT

THE BIRTH OF JESUS

In the little town of Nazareth in Galilee there lived a good and gentle young woman named Mary. She was engaged to a local carpenter named Joseph, a fine, kindly man whose family was descended from King David.

One day, as Mary went about her household duties, she had a surprising visitor. An angel named Gabriel suddenly appeared before her. "Hail, Mary," he said, "the Lord is with you."

Mary was puzzled, for she did not understand what the angel's visit could mean.

"Do not be afraid, Mary," said the angel, "for you are to have a son, and His name will be Jesus. He will be the son of the Most High God, and He will be a king whose kingdom will never end."

"How can this be?" asked Mary, greatly worried. "I have no husband."

"The Holy Spirit will come to you," answered the angel, "so that God's power will be with you, for the child will be the Son of God."

"I am God's servant," said Mary quietly. "May it happen as you have said."

And then the angel left her.

Joseph was troubled at Mary's news and wondered whether he should still marry her. Then an angel appeared to him in a dream and reassured him, "Do not be afraid to take Mary for your wife. God's Holy Spirit has come to her, and she will have a son who is to be called Jesus—for He will save people from their sins."

(The name "Jesus" is in fact the Greek form of the Hebrew name "Joshua" and means "saviour").

Now Palestine in those days was part of the Roman Empire, and some time after the appearance of the angel to Mary and Joseph, the Roman Emperor, Caesar Augustus, issued an order. He commanded that everyone should be "enrolled", which meant that there would be a sort of census or numbering of the people. To do this, each person was to return to his home town or city to register himself.

For Joseph this meant a long journey of about 72 miles, from Nazareth in Galilee southwards to Bethlehem in Judea. Bethlehem had been the home of Ruth and Boaz, and also the birthplace of King David.

The journey would be a long and tiring walk, for, apart from a donkey, there was no other means of transport. Joseph had to make careful preparations for the journey, especially as Mary was going with him and would soon be having her baby.

They were both very tired by the time they reached Bethlehem. What a busy town it was! Everywhere was hustle and bustle, for crowds of people had come for the enrolment. There seemed to be no room anywhere for the weary travellers from Bethlehem to stay the night. Joseph was anxious about Mary, and became worried when the last innkeeper they asked told him that he had not a single room left vacant in the inn; he was completely full with visitors.

Then, no doubt, he looked again at Mary and saw how tired

she was, and he took pity on her. "There is the stable where the animals are kept," he suggested. "You could shelter there for the night if you wish."

Joseph was ready to take anything, for he could see that Mary was not fit to travel much further, and he readily agreed. At least the stable would provide shelter, and they could find a warm corner and lie down on some of the animals' straw.

Thankfully, they went into the stable, and during the night, with no one looking except the animals, Mary's baby was born. She wrapped Him up in strips of cloth, called swaddling clothes, which was the usual custom in that part of the world. There was no cradle where she might lay her baby, so she put Him gently in a manger where hay was kept to feed the animals.

It was a strange arrival for the Son of God. Kings are not normally born in stables; they are born in palaces amid rich pomp and splendour, but when God allowed Jesus to be born in this humble way in the stable, He was showing that He was sympathetic to the poor and was the King of *all* people, not only of the rich and important. By living as the poorest, Jesus would show how He really understood them and took their part.

In the countryside, outside Bethlehem, a group of shepherds were looking after their sheep on the night when Jesus was born.

The work of shepherds was important and dangerous, since not only had they to lead their flocks to pasture, they had also to protect them from any wild animals that came prowling around. To this end, they stayed with their sheep both day and night, and when the flock was herded into the fold, often the shepherd himself would lie across the opening of the doorway, so that nothing could get into the pen without his knowledge.

On this clear night, the Bethlehem shepherds wrapped their cloaks around them against the cold and talked among themselves. Perhaps they remembered that King David had once been a shepherd boy himself. They gazed up at the night sky and saw many bright stars, but they were used to that.

Suddenly there seemed to be much more light than usual. The whole field was lit up with a brilliant radiance, and in the midst of it the shepherds saw the figure of an angel. They were terrified and covered their faces.

"Do not be afraid," said the angel, "for I have brought you good news which will bring great joy to all the people. This very day in Bethlehem, the city of David, the Saviour of the world has been born. He is Christ the Lord."

The shepherds were amazed; they could hardly take in such an important announcement and naturally they wondered why the angel had come to them with this great news.

The angel continued, "As a sign to prove it to you, you will find the baby wrapped in swaddling clothes and lying in a manger."

Hardly had the angel's words died away, than the whole sky surrounding the spot was filled with a multitude of angels. "Glory to God in the highest," they sang, "and on earth peace to men with whom He is pleased."

Then the angels went away, and the earth grew quiet and still. Only the stars were left in the sky.

The shepherds looked at one another in wonder. Was it true? Could they be dreaming? The Messiah, the Saviour of the world, here in Bethlehem? and in a *stable*? It did not seem possible.

Then one of the shepherds said, "Come on, let's go and see this

"Lord, now let your servant depart in peace."

"The Wise Men fell down and worshipped Him."

wonderful thing which the Lord has told us about through His angel."

They hurried off, over the hills, and into Bethlehem. Almost certainly they left one of their number behind to take care of the sheep.

But where in Bethlehem should they look? From what the angel had said, the shepherds knew that it would be useless to look in any rich or important house, for the baby would be lying in a manger. Any rich house would provide a proper cot. Mangers were found only in stables, so they must look for a stable if they wanted to find the new-born king.

When at last they looked in at the stable belonging to the inn, there they found the new baby, and they knelt down and worshipped Him in wonder.

Mary, His mother, and Joseph, her husband, were gazing fondly down at Him. The shepherds told them all the angel had said, but Mary already knew something about her wonderful baby, for the angel Gabriel had told her whom He was to be. So she kept silent, but thought a great deal about the wonderful happening.

The shepherds, however, were greatly excited about the event, and they could not keep quiet about it. They returned to their sheep, singing praises to God. They had heard the angel with their own ears, they had seen the baby with their own eyes; however much other people might find it hard to believe that God's Son had been born in a stable, they knew that it was true.

Forty days after Jesus was born, Mary and Joseph, according to the law, took Him to the temple in Jerusalem to be presented to God. On these occasions, it was necessary to present an offering, which would normally be a lamb. Poor people, however, such as Mary and Joseph, were allowed to offer two turtle-doves or two young pigeons instead.

In Jerusalem at that time, there lived a good man whose name was Simeon. He was a God-fearing man, and it had been revealed to him that he would not die until he had seen the true Christ. ("Christ" comes from the Greek word meaning "anointed"; and "Messiah" from a Hebrew word meaning the same thing.) It happened that he was in the temple when Mary and Joseph came in to present Jesus. As soon as Simeon saw Jesus he knew who He was and came forward at once.

Simeon took the baby in his arms and said, "Lord, now let your servant go in peace, for I have seen the Saviour with my own eyes."

Mary and Joseph were amazed at the things which Simeon said, for they were only slowly realizing the wonderul truth about their baby. Simeon blessed them too, and then he told Mary that Jesus would be the salvation of many in Israel, but that many people would speak against Him, and that she would suffer much sorrow.

THE VISIT OF THE WISE MEN

SOME time after the birth of Jesus, a group of rather important-looking men arrived in Jerusalem and began asking questions. They were men who studied the stars and their meanings, and were known as astrologers, or sometimes as "magi", or just "wise men".

They had come on a long journey from the east, from where, before they had begun their travels, they had seen a very bright new star in the sky. From their knowledge, they believed that this star meant the brith of the long-promised new King of the Jews. So, wanting to find out more, they had set off on their camels to follow the star. (The Bible does not say that there were three of them, but it has always been generally thought that this was so because they brought three gifts.)

When the star had led them as far as Jerusalem, the wise men began to ask people if this was the place to which they should come to find the new king. Surely Jerusalem was a suitable place for a king to be born, they thought. "Where is He who is born King of the Jews?" they asked. "We have seen His star in the east, and have travelled here to worship Him."

But no one in Jerusalem knew anything about a king being born there. So far as they knew, the only king in the area was Herod.

The news about the wise men's questionings reached the ears of King Herod, and he did not like the sound of it at all. He was a very jealous character, and he wanted no rivals to his throne or his power.

"A new king?" he thought, and became full of mistrust and suspicion. Not only was he troubled, but all the people of Jerusalem were troubled too, for when Herod was upset one never knew what he might do. He had killed many of the leading men of the city not long before, while suffering from a fit of fear and jealousy. He really could not be trusted an inch.

Herod summoned together all the chief priests and teachers of the law and asked them what they knew about it. "Where will this Messiah, this King of the Jews, be born?" he asked in a pleasant, interested way.

They knew the answer to that one. It had been foretold by the prophet Micah hundreds of years earlier. He had written, "And you, Bethlehem, in the land of Judah, are not the least of the cities of Judah, for from you there will come a ruler who will guide the people of Israel." That could only mean the Messiah.

"Bethlehem," thought Herod. "Something must be done about this without delay." So he summoned the wise men from the east to a secret conference. He found out from them at what time the star had appeared, and then he sent them off to Bethlehem to look for the new king whose birth seemed such a threat to him.

"Go and search very carefully for the young child," he told them, "and as soon as you have found him, come back here and let me know; for I would like to go and worship him too." Of course, Herod had no intention of going to worship a rival king.

All he wanted was to find out where the child was so that he could have him removed as a rival to the throne and make sure that he, Herod, was the only king the Jews recognized.

The wise men left Jerusalem. They were pleased to see the star again and to follow it until it came to rest over Bethlehem, and over a certain house there. Now that the enrolling and the census was over, Bethlehem was no longer full of visitors, and Mary and Joseph would have had no difficulty in finding somewhere better than a stable to live in and to bring up the new baby.

Joyfully the wise men went into the house where they saw the young child Jesus and His mother, and they knelt down and worshipped Him, happy that thier long search was over.

Then, as it was the custom not to approach a monarch without bringing a gift, they presented their gifts to the new King of the Jews. They were royal gifts—of gold, frankincense and myrrh—costly products of the countries from which the men had ome. Frankincense was the resin from the bark of the terebinth tree; it had a pleasant smell and was used by priests in temple worship to make fragrant smoke at the altar. Myrrh was a sweet-smelling gum and was used as a perfume, in medicine and in anointing oils. They were all most suitable gifts for a king.

While in Bethlehem the wise men had a dream, which through their learning they were able to interpret, and in it God warned them not to go back to King Herod, as he had requested; so they went back home another way, slipping quietly across the borders of Israel.

When the wise men did not return to Jerusalem, Herod realized that he had been tricked, and he flew into a furious rage. He gave orders that all baby boys in Bethlehem, who were two years old and under, were to be killed at once. They way, he thought, he would be sure to kill the new king among them.

Meanwhile, after the wise men had departed, Joseph also had a dream in which an angel appeared to him and said, "Get up quickly, and take the young child, and Mary His mother, and escape into Egypt, for Herod is looking for the child in order to kill Him."

So that night, under cover of darkness, Joseph did as the angel had bidden him, and with Mary and Jesus he fled into Egypt, out of the range of Herod's power. So Herod's wicked plot was foiled, and there they remained until the day that Herod died.

Then the angel appeared to Joseph in another dream and said, "It is quite safe for you to take the child and His mother back to Israel now, for those who were searching for Him, to kill Him, are themselves now dead."

At first Joseph thought of returning to Judah, perhaps to Bethlehem, but when he heard that Archelaus was now king there, in place of his father Herod, he was afraid, for Archelaus was nearly as suspicious and cruel as his father had been. So Joseph went instead to Galilee and there he, Mary and Jesus settled in Nazareth which lay in lower Galilee on the slopes of the Lebanon mountain range. Like Bethlehem it too was a quite unimportant town that was never to be forgotten because of its links with Jesus. And so it was in Nazareth that Jesus spent His boyhood.

Jesus As a Boy

Jesus was to live in Nazareth until He was about thirty years old, and this is why, although He was born in Bethelehem, He is often known as Jesus of Nazareth. The Bible tells us that He "increased in wisdom and stature, and in favour with God and man." In other words, He grew, not only in height, but also in wisdom, knowledge and learning, and with God's blessing, the people loved Him and respected Him.

As a boy, He would help Mary in the everyday tasks of their humble home and also work with Joseph in making articles of wood in their carpenter's shop. There He would become a skilled worker in wood, learning to make roofs, doors, beds, chests, tables and chairs. Carpenters also made agricultural implements, such as ploughs, yokes and threshing instruments, so there would be plenty to keep the boy Jesus busy in the small farming community.

He would also be taught in the local synagogue by the rabbi or scribes, where He would learn about the Jewish law. There would be no books, and education consisted chiefly of repeating words and so learning the facts by heart. Every Sabbath He would attend the synagogue for worship, and when He grew up, He would read aloud the scriptures there as would Joseph and all the other boys and their fathers.

In His free time, He probably wandered about the country-side, where many of the things He saw, He remembered and used later in His teaching when He grew up and told people stories, or parables, about the familiar things of life—cornfields, sowers, vineyards, sheep and shepherds. His own knowledge made the stories very real and appealing to His listeners and helped them to see how the stories made sense in their own lives and dealt with their common problems.

Every year Mary and Joseph used to journey to Jerusalem to join with hundreds of other pilgrims who flocked there from all over Palestine to celebrate the Passover.

When a Jewish boy was twelve years of age, he had to undergo preparation to become an adult in the religious community and to take his full part in the religious life of the village. He would then become what was known as a "son of the law" and be expected to obey its rules. From that time onward, he would no longer be looked upon as a child, but would be considered as a full member of the Jewish church.

So, when Jesus was twelve, Mary and Joseph decided that the time had come for Him to go with them on their visit to the festival at Jerusalem. Because of all that it meant, it would be a very special visit for Jesus.

People from the same town or village would often make the journey together, walking along the rough highways and sleeping out at nights on the way. They travelled in groups for safety, for there were robbers and other possible dangers. It was a long journey, and they would be on the road for several days. The young boys would find it a very exciting adventure, and would be thrilled when they saw Jerusalem for the first time. They would then take part in ceremonies which they would remember all their lives.

When the festival was over the people started to walk back home again, but on this particular occasion, Jesus stayed behind in Jerusalem, and did not set off back with His parents, although they did not realize this. No doubt they thought He was somewhere in the great company of people walking back— perhaps with relatives or friends, or with other boys of His own age, racing on ahead, or stopping to explore.

After they had been walking for a day, they made an evening halt, and it was then that Mary and Joseph found that Jesus was nowhere to be seen in the company. Where could He be? Anxiously they asked around among the other travellers, but no one could recall seeing Him that day. Mary and Joseph became very worried and decided that the best thing to do was to retrace their steps to Jerusalem, in the hope that they would find him on the way.

The next day, they set off back to the city, asking everyone they met whether they had seen Jesus, but no one could help them. At last they reached Jerusalem itself and began looking in the city. It was now three days since they had started out on the homeward journey. After much worried searching, they finally found Jesus in the temple itself. He was sitting with a group of Jewish teachers, listening to them and asking them questions. The teachers were amazed at Jesus's understanding and at His intelligent questions and answers.

Mary and Joseph, too, were astonished when they discovered where Jesus was and what He was doing. Mary said to Him, "My son, why did you stay behind like this? Why have you treated us so? We have been most worried trying to find you."

Jesus was surprised—not that they had come back for Him, but at their not knowing where He would be. He had thought they would have known He would be in the temple. "Why did you need to look for me?" He asked. "Did you not know that I had to be in My Father's house and about My Father's business?"

By His "Father", He meant God; for even at that early age, He understood His special relationship with God the Father.

Mary and Joseph did not fully understand His answer, but Jesus then went back to Nazareth with them, and was obedient to them, thus showing His love and respect for them both.

Mary thought deeply about what had happened. She remembered the words of the angel Gabriel before Jesus was born, that her child was to be the Son of God; and also how the aged Simeon in the temple had called Jesus "the Saviour". She must have wondered what the future had in store.

JESUS CALLS HIS FOLLOWERS

WHEN Jesus was about thirty years old, He knew He was ready to start His work. He chose a band of twelve ordinary men as followers, to help him in this.

These followers came from the same area as Jesus Himself. The first one to be called was named Andrew. He was with another man when Jesus was first pointed out to him as someone very special. Andrew and his companion at once set off after Jesus, following Him at a short distance. Jesus turned and saw them.

"What are you looking for?" He asked.

"Where do you live, teacher?" they asked Him.

"Come and see," said Jesus; so they went with Him, saw where He was living, and spent the rest of the day with Him.

Andrew was so impressed with Jesus that he immediately went and found his own brother, Simon. "Simon, we have found the Messiah," he said, and he took Simon to Jesus.

Jesus looked at Simon and saw what was in him. He knew what a great leader this man could be, and He said, "From now on you will be called Cephas" (which means "a rock" and is the same word as "Peter". This is why Simon is often referred to as "Simon Peter" or simply as "Peter"). Because Andrew brought his brother to Jesus, he was really the first Christian missionary.

Both Andrew and Simon Peter were simple fishermen. They worked in their fishing business with two other brothers whose names were James and John, and whose father was named Zebedee. James and John became disciples too, and three of these first four (Peter, James and John) were to become specially close to Jesus.

After this first call, these four attached themselves to Jesus as disciples, or learners, and when they realized that He was the Messiah, they were ready to leave their homes, their business and everything, and to follow Him completely.

It happened that Jesus was walking along the shores of the Sea of Galilee one day when He again saw the fishermen at their work.

The Lake or Sea of Galilee was also called the Sea of Tiberias because the town of Tiberias lay on its western shore. It is a low, freshwater lake, measuring some 13 miles long by about six and a half miles wide. Much of Jesus's ministry was to take place in the towns and countryside around the lake, in places like Capernaum and Bethsaida.

The people were crowding around Jesus, and wanting to hear what He had to say about God and His Kingdom. Jesus saw two boats pulled up to the shore, one of which belonged to Simon Peter. He got into it and asked Simon to push it out a little way so that He could sit in it and teach the people on the shore. They could all see and hear Him more easily that way.

When He had finished speaking, He said to Simon Peter, "Push your boat out further into the deep water and then let down your nets for a catch."

"But master," said Simon, "we have been out all night and

have caught nothing. Still, if You say so, we will obey."

When the fishermen let down their nets they caught such a great number of fish that the nets were almost broken with the weight. They had to signal to their partners in the other boat to come and help them. Both boats were soon so full of fish that they were about to sink.

Simon Peter was so impressed that he felt himself much too unworthy to remain in the presence of such a powerful person as Jesus. He said to Jesus, "Depart from me, for I am a sinful man."

"Don't be afraid," said Jesus, "for from now on, all your life you will be catching people not fish."

On another day, when Jesus was in Galilee, He called a man named Philip to follow Him. Philip came from Bethsaida, the place where Andrew and Simon Peter lived, and he brought another future disciple, Nathanael, also sometimes called Bartholomew, to Jesus.

"We have found the one whom Moses and the prophets wrote about," Philip told Nathanael. "He is Jesus, the son of Joseph, from Nazareth."

Nathanael was doubtful. "Can anything good come from Nazareth?" he asked.

To which Philip replied simply, "Come and see."

When Jesus saw Nathanael coming towards Him, He said that here was an honest and true Israelite.

"How do you know me?" asked Nathanael, and Jesus replied that He had seen Nathanael under a fig-tree before Philip had even called him. Nathanael was quite astonished.

Another time Jesus saw a man who was a tax-collector sitting in his tax office, and said to him, "Follow me," and the man followed Him. He was Matthew, also called Levi. Tax-collectors, or publicans, who collected taxes on behalf of the Romans were much despised as they often took more money than they were entitled to. But Jesus did not despise anyone, and He always had a special care for those who were despised and outcast by others.

The full list of the inner band of twelve is—Simon Peter, Andrew, James, John, Philip, Nathanael, Matthew, Thomas, another James (son of Alphaeus), Thaddaeus, another Simon (the Zealot), and Judas Iscariot.

THE STORY OF

THE GOOD SAMARITAN

JESUS became well known as a teacher, but there were always those who wanted to prove themselves cleverer than He was.

One day when Jesus was teaching, a lawyer came up to Him, hoping to trap Him with a clever question. "What shall I do to gain eternal life?" he asked Jesus.

Jesus replied, "What do the scriptures tell you? How do you interpret them?"

The lawyer replied, "Love God with all your heart, with all your soul, with all your mind and with all your strength; and love your neighbour as you love yourself."

"Quite right," said Jesus. "Do that and you will live."

The lawyer, somewhat taken aback, tried to save face by asking another question. Perhaps his conscience pricked him and he wanted to justify his own lack of love.

"But who *is* my neighbour?" he asked, looking puzzled.

Instead of answering directly, Jesus told him a story as HHe often did when He was teaching. A story is a very good way of explaining a point, because people remember stories far more easily than they remember plain facts and they can repeat the stories to other people.

Jesus's stories had a deeper meaning than most and are called parables, which means "earthly stories with a heavenly meaning". This is the story He told to the lawyer.

Once there was a man who was going on a journey from Jerusalem to Jericho, a distance of about 17 miles. The way lay along a rocky, lonely and dangerous road infested by murderous brigands.

Suddenly a gang of robbers sprang out from behind some rocks and attacked the man. They tore off his clothes and beat him up, and then left him half dead, lying on the road in the blazing sun. His wounds were very painful, and flies bothered him and he was very thirsty, but there was no one anywhere near to come to his aid. His plight was terrible.

A while later it happened that a priest was travelling along the same road. When the wounded man heard footsteps, he opened his eyes, and when he saw that the figure was a priest, he felt a little happier. Surely here was someone who would help?

The priest saw the man, but he did not stop; he just hurried by on the other side. Perhaps he told himself he hadn't time to stop, as he was on important business for the temple, perhaps he was afraid robbers might attack him too if he stopped so he kept on going.

Shortly afterwards, there were more footsteps, and the wounded man's hopes rose again when he saw that a Levite was coming that way. A Levite was a helper in the temple, and he might well be expected to be the sort of man who would help someone in distress.

But no, the Levite looked at the wounded man, and then he too hurried by on the other side of the road.

Once more the man heard the footsteps die away and the road became quiet and lonely again. He felt desperate.

"After three days they found Him in the Temple, with
the doctors, both hearing them and asking them questions."

"Simon Peter and Andrew, come! Follow Me!"

Before long, the man heard more footsteps of a different kind. This time a donkey was coming down the road with a man on his back. The wounded man was very disappointed to see that the rider was a Samaritan.

The Jews and the Samaritans had been enemies for a very long time. The Jews of Judah in the south hated the Samaritans who lived in Samaria in the north, for the Samaritans were a mixed race and were thought to be not wholly loyal to Israel's God.

The wounded man felt pretty sure he could not expect any help from a Samaritan, but, to his great surprise, the donkey stopped and the rider dismounted. He came over to the wounded man and looked kindly at him. He felt sorry and wondered what he could do to help. His own safety did not seem to worry him.

Then he went back to his donkey and brought over some oil and some wine which he had with him. These he put on the man's wounds, to act as antiseptic and ointment, and bandaged him up. He probably had to tear up some of his own clothes in order to make strips for bandages as it is unlikely that he carried any with him.

Next he lifted up the wounded man gently and put him on his own donkey. Then, with the Samaritan walking at the side and holding the wounded man, they slowly made their way until they came to an inn.

The Samaritan asked the innkeeper for a room, and led the man to it and took care of him there. He put him to bed, bathed his wounds with water and bandaged them up afresh, and gave the man some food and drink. Then he made him comfortable and left him to sleep.

The following day the Samaritan had to continue his journey, but before he went, he wondered what else he could do for the wounded man who would have to remain resting at the inn for quite some time until he was well enough to return to his family.

He took out two coins and gave them to the innkeeper. "Look after him," he told the innkeeper, "and if it should cost you any more than this, I will pay you the extra amount when I come back this way again."

Having finished his story, Jesus turned to the lawyer and asked, "Which of the three passers-by do you think acted like a neighbour to the man attacked by the robbers?"

"The one who showed pity and acted kindly to him," replied the lawyer.

"Then go and do the same," said Jesus.

Jesus Blesses The Children

One day Jesus and His disciples were going to Capernaum, and on the way the disciples were arguing among themselves as to who was the greatest and most important of them.

When they got indoors, Jesus questioned them about this. "What were you all arguing about on the way here?" He asked. But the disciples would not answer, because they were all feeling somewhat ashamed of themselves. However, Jesus knew, without needing any answer from them, and He sat down and called them all to Him.

"If you want to be first and really important," He said, "you must put yourself last. You must be ready to be the servant of everyone else. Those are the people who are truly great."

Now there was a little child listening to all this—perhaps he was the child who lived in the house—and Jesus put His arm round him, and said, "The greatest in the Kingdom of Heaven is one who is as humble as this little child. Anyone who welcomes a child is welcoming Me. For he who is least among you is the greatest."

Jesus was trying to explain to the disciples that God's Kingdom has very different standards from the world. Riches and power do not make anyone great in God's eyes. Being loving, generous, humble and forgiving are far more important, and people with these qualities are the ones who are truly great. Such people may seem as unimportant as a child to the world, but in God's Kingdom they are the ones who are the greatest.

Jesus loved children and as He went about He noticed them playing. Like children today, they liked to pretend they were grown-up, and sometimes they would play at weddings or funerals and fall out over their games.

On one occasion some people brought a number of children to Jesus, knowing how He loved them. They wanted Him to put His hands on them and bless them.

When the disciples saw this, they rebuked the people and tried to send the children away, for they did not want Jesus to be troubled by them. No doubt they thought that childen were not important enough to claim His attention.

Jesus, however, thought very differently. He was never troubled by people coming to Him, no matter how young—or how old—they might be. He would never turn anyone away.

He did not like the way the disciples were dealing with the children, and He called them back to Him. Then He said, "Let the children come to Me, and do not try to stop them, for the Kingdom of God belongs to such children as these. I tell you that whoever does not receive the Kingdom of God in the same spirit as a child, will never enter into it."

He did not mean that people should be childish and never to grow up in their ideas. He meant that they should receive God's Kingdom in a child-like spirit—that is, one of humble, loving trust. This can apply to anyone of any age.

Then Jesus took the children in His arms and put His hands on each of them and blessed them.

Jesus Calms a Storm
And Walks On Water

On the evening of the day when Jesus had been telling the story of the sower to a crowd of people, He said to the disciples, "Let us cross to the other side of the lake."

So they left the crowd, and got into the little boat in which Jesus had been sitting to teach, and they began to row across.

The lake was the Sea of Galilee, which lies low about 600 feet below sea-level. All around there are hills, with deep ravines and gorges, and these act as funnels, drawing down the winds from the mountains. From time to time, these winds lash the waters into a great fury, making it dangerous for small boats.

Suddenly, as Jesus and the disciples were crossing, one of these great strong winds blew up, tossing the little boat about and hurling in lots of water, putting them all in great danger of sinking or overturning.

The disciples were panic-stricken, even though some of them were experienced sailors. They turned to Jesus and found Him in the back of the boat—fast asleep, for He was tired after being with the crowds all day.

It seemed as though the little boat would be completely swamped by the raging waves, and the terrified disciples rushed to wake Jesus up. "Master! Master! We are going to perish!" they cried. "Don't you care?"

Calmly Jesus got up and said to the wind, "Be quiet!" and to the waves He said, "Peace, be still."

And there was at once a great calm.

"Why were you so frightened?" asked Jesus of the disciples. "Haven't you any faith?"

The disciples looked at one another in awe and wonder and said, "What sort of man is this—that even the winds and the sea obey Him?"

Another time, by Galilee, Jesus asked the disciples to get into a boat and row across to Bethsaida at the other side of the lake. Meanwhile, He sent the crowd of people home and went up on the hillside by Himself to pray.

By evening time, the disciples in their little boat were far out on the lake, and were being tossed about somewhat, for it was a windy night and the sea was choppy.

Sometime between 3 am and 6 am, when they had been rowing for about three miles the disciples looked out and saw a figure walking towards them on the water. They were terrified and screamed with fear. "It's a ghost!" they cried, their voices trembling.

Then the familiar and beloved voice of Jesus said, "Do not be afraid. It is I."

Now Peter, confident and enthusiastic as always, spoke up and said, "Lord, if it is really You, tell me to come to You on the water."

"Come," said Jesus.

So Peter got out of the boat and began to walk on the water towards Jesus. But his faith did not last for long, and when he saw what a strong wind there was, he grew afraid—and as soon as he stopped trusting Jesus, he began to sink. "Lord! Save me!" he cried out.

Jesus reached out and grabbed hold of his hand and said, "What little faith you have! Why did you doubt?"

Then they both climbed into the boat, and the wind died down, the raging waves grew calm and the storm faded away.

The disciples turned to Jesus in awe saying, "Truly, You are the Son of God."

THE FEEDING OF THE

FIVE THOUSAND

CROWDS followed Jesus everywhere, for they saw His miracles and heard His teaching, and they wanted to see and hear more. He was becoming quite famous.

One day, near the time for the Passover Festival, when many Galileans came to Jerusalem, a huge crowd followed Jesus up a hillside. Jesus had been hoping to take His disciples away for a short rest, and they had gone to this quiet place by boat. The crowds, however, had followed round the lake, on foot, and many were already on the hillside when Jesus arrived.

Among them was a young boy whose mother had given him a picnic meal to take out with him. Perhaps he had told her that he was going to see and hear Jesus, the great teacher, and she knew he would probably be away all day. But there were few other people in the crowd, if any, who had thought to bring food with them, even to give to their children.

Jesus sat down on the top of a hill, and looked round at the hundreds of people gathered about Him. He felt sorry for them, for He knew they must be getting hungry and they were all a long way from home.

"It's getting late," said the disciples. "Send them all away so that they can go into the towns and villages and buy themselves something to eat."

Jesus knew He could feed the multitude, but He wanted to test the disciples; so He turned to Philip and said, "Where can we buy enough bread out here in the open to feed this great crowd?"

Philip said, "Even if they each had only a little, it would take at least 200 silver coins."

No one had that sort of money on them, for one silver coin was an average wage for a day's work, and 200 such coins would be equal to more than six months' wages.

Then another disciple, Andrew, who was Simon Peter's brother, noticed the boy with the picnic meal. "There is a lad here," said Andrew, "who has brought with him five loaves of barley bread and two small fish—but they won't be anything like enough for all these people." Andrew and the other disciples began to look worried.

There seemed to be no one else with any food at all.

"Make them all sit down," said Jesus.

So they all sat down in groups on the green grass; there were about 100 people in some groups and about fifty in others, and in their beautifully coloured robes, in the sunshine, they looked rather like flower beds in a garden in the summertime.

Then Jesus took the five loaves which the boy had offered, gave thanks to God, and broke the loaves and gave them to the disciples to distribute among the people. Then He did the same with the fish.

There were more than 5,000 people in the crowd and the disciples went to each little group, giving food to everyone in it.

The wonderful thing was that no matter how much the disciples gave out, the supply they carried was never finished. Everyone ate and soon they had all had as much as they wanted and felt completely satisfied and contented.

Jesus did not believe in wasting any of God's good gifts, so He said to the disciples, "Now gather up all the pieces that remain, so there shall be no waste."

Each of the disciples took a large basket and went round collecting up all the scraps they could find; and each filled his basket. This meant that, after at least 5,000 people had eaten their fill, there were still twelve baskets of food remaining from what had been one boy's picnic lunch of five small loves and two little fishes.

The people were all astonished, for they had seen the miracle with their own eyes. They said to one another, "Surely this is the great prophet who was to come into the world."

The boy who had given up his picnic must have had a wonderful story to tell his parents when he got back home!

JESUS THE HEALER

JESUS soon became well known for His works of healing and people came to him from far and near to be cured of their illnesses.

One day, after he had been teaching in Galilee, there came to Him a man who was suffering from a terrible skin disease called leprosy. Today it is possible to cure this disease, but in Jesus's day there was no hope at all. A leper had to keep right away from the other people because the law regarded him as unclean. No one, knowing him to be a leper, dare approach him, but if anyone accidentally did come near him, the leper had to cry out "Unclean!" and people would back hastily away in case they caught the disease.

Thus lepers, as well as being ill, led a very lonely life, entirely cut off from human company, except for other lepers.

But Jesus did not shun them, for He never shunned anyone in trouble. When this leper came and asked to be healed, Jesus stretched out His hand and touched him. The leper said, "If you will, you can make me clean."

"I will," said Jesus. "Be clean," and immediately the disease went from the man.

Jesus instructed him not to spread the news of how he had been healed, because He did not want people to come and proclaim Him as the Messiah yet; but told the man to go to a priest to be examined, and make an offering to prove that he was cured. This was as the law of Israel commanded.

However the man was naturally so excited that he told everyone he met, and the result was that Jesus could not go into the towns for a while and had to stay in the desert.

Jesus often made blind men see again, and one day, outside Jericho, there sat a blind man by the roadside. His name was Bartimaeus.

Many blind people have a keen sense of hearing, and Bartimaeus would be able to recognize the familiar sounds of people and animals passing by. He had also heard about the great healer, Jesus of Nazareth, and perhaps he thought about Him a great deal.

One day he heard the noise of a great crowd of people coming along the road, such a noise as he had never heard before. He could tell, from the scraps of conversation he heard, that Jesus was with them. He could not see Jesus, of course, but he wondered if Jesus could see him. He decided to call out and attract His attention. "Jesus, son of David, have mercy on me!" he cried.

People in the crowd scolded him. "Be quiet!"they said.

But Bartimaeus cried out all the more loudly, "Son of David, have mercy on me!" Calling Him "son of David" showed that Bartimaeus had given some thought as to who Jesus really was.

Jesus stopped and said to the people, "Call him."

So they called to him and said, "Take heart; get up, for Jesus is calling you."

Bartimaeus sprang up and made his way to Jesus.

"What do you want me to do?" Jesus asked.

"Lord, that I might receive my sight," answered Bartimaeus.

"Go your way," said Jesus, "your faith has made you whole."

And at once Bartimaeus was able to see, and he followed Jesus along the road.

Another time, Jesus healed a man in Jerusalem. There was a pool in that city with five porches or porticoes; it was called the Pool of Bethesda. This pool, with its five porticoes has since been discovered by archaeologists, down below the level of present-day Jerusalem.

A large number of sick people used to lie in the porches waiting for the waters to become stirred up or "troubled". This happened from time to time, perhaps caused by the bubbling up of an underground stream, but the people believed that the first to go into the water when it was bubbling would be cured of his or her illness.

When Jesus went there, He saw, among the crowds of sick people, one man who had been ill for thirty-eight years. He was lying on a mat, and seemed to be the sort of person who had lost all will to live.

"Do you really want to get well?" asked Jesus, stopping beside him.

"Sir," replied the man, "I have no one to help me into the pool when the water is troubled, and while I am struggling to get in on my own, someone else gets there first, and I lose my chance."

Obviously the man needed encouragement from somebody.

"Get up, pick up your mat, and walk!" said Jesus to him. Immediately the man found he could stand, and he picked up his mat and started to walk.

All this, like many of the other miracles that Jesus did, took place on the Sabbath day. On this day, Jewish people are forbidden by the laws of their religion to work. Some of the most strictly religious people at the time began to criticize Jesus for healing on this day, and He soon found He had enemies.

But He continued His work. It soon became clear that He could heal very seriously sick people. One such case was Jairus's daughter.

Jairus was a rich man who lived near the Sea of Galilee. He was an official of the local synagogue. He had a daughter who was twelve, and she was ill – so ill that it seemed that she would not recover.

When Jairus saw Jesus with a large crowd around Him, he ran towards Him and begged, "My daughter is very ill. Please come and lay your hands on her and make her well."

So Jesus set off towards Jairus's house, and a great number of people went too, crowding and jostling Him on all sides.

In this crowd was a woman who had had an illness which caused severe bleeding for twelve years. She had spent all her money on doctors and medicines, but instead of getting better, she grew worse. She had heard about Jesus, and she thought to herself, "If I can only just touch the hem of His robes, I shall be made well."

So she pushed her way through the crowd and touched His cloak, and she knew she had been made well right away.

Now there was nothing magic about Jesus's clothes, but He could tell the difference between the jostling of the crowd and someone reaching out to Him in real need. "Who touched Me?" He asked.

The disciples were amazed at this question, and they said, "Look how hard the crowd is pressing around You, and yet You ask, "Who touched Me?"

But Jesus knew that someone had touched Him deliberately, and He looked to see who it was. The poor woman, who had hoped not to be noticed, now came forward and fell at Jesus's feet, trembling, and poured out the whole story.

"Don't be afraid," said Jesus gently, "your faith has made you well. Go home in peace."

While He was saying this, some messengers came from Jairus's house and said, "Don't trouble the Master any more, for your daughter has just died."

Jesus ignored this and said to Jairus, "Don't be afraid, just believe, and your daughter will be made well." And He pressed on.

When they reached Jairus's house, there was a terrible noise going on. Everyone was crying and mourning for the child. "Why do you make this noise?" asked Jesus. "The child is not dead, she is asleep."

But they laughed at Him, for they knew, or thought they knew, that she was really and truly dead.

Then Jesus put them all outside and took with Him only the child's parents and Peter, James and John, and He went into the little girl's room. He took her by the hand and said, "Get up, little girl." And her life returned and she started to walk around.

"Give her something to eat," said Jesus, as He returned her to her overjoyed parents.

JESUS ENTERS JERUSALEM

IT was Passover time, a busy time in the city, when thousands of Jews were going up to the temple in Jerusalem to keep the festival, the great feast which commemorated the nation's deliverance from Egypt.

Jesus and His disciples were on their way to Jerusalem too, but the disciples could sense that this time their journey had a much more serious feel to it. Although they did not realize it at the time, this was the start of Jesus's last week of life on earth.

Jesus was very set and determined and walked on a little ahead of them. The people following were afraid, for they knew that the rulers wanted to seize Jesus, and by going into Jerusalem they felt that He was heading for certain capture.

Jesus took His twelve disciples aside and said to them, "We are going to Jerusalem where the chief priests and rulers will condemn the Son of Man to death, and hand Him over to the Gentiles (non-Jews) who will mock, whip and crucify Him. But after three days He will rise again."

He was talking about Himself and what was to happen, but the disciples did not understand.

As they drew near to the city, they came to Bethphage, which was about one-and-a-half miles outside Jerusalem, and near to the Mount of Olives. Here Jesus gave the disciples some special

"Suffer little children to come unto Me."

"The little boy must have been proud and happy, too, when
Andrew took the basket."

instructions. "Go into the village over there," He said, "and you will find a colt (a young donkey) tied up, on which no one has ever ridden. Untie it and bring it to me. If anyone asks what you are doing, you are to say, 'The Master needs it and will return it at once.' Then the man will allow you to bring it to me."

The disciples went and found the colt just as Jesus had said, and as they were untying it, the owners asked what they were doing. The disciples replied as Jesus had told them, and the owners said no more.

When the disciples brought the animal to Jesus, some of them threw their cloaks over it, and Jesus mounted to ride the rest of the way into Jerusalem.

Now the people who had been present when Jesus had brought Lazarus to life again had told many people about what had happened. So when they heard that Jesus was coming to Jerusalem, a great crowd went out to meet Him.

The Pharisees were most put out at this, and they said to one another in frustration, "You see, we can do nothing; the whole world is following Him."

The great crowd wanted to honour and praise Jesus as their king. Many knew that it was customary to put down a carpet for a king to walk on, and so they spread their brightly coloured cloaks in the path of Jesus to make a carpet for Him, as a gesture of respect. Other people climbed palm trees along the route, and cut down branches to wave or to spread along the road.

"Hosanna!" they cried, "Praise to the son of David! Blessed is He who comes in the name of the Lord! Praise God!"

There were crowds in front and crowds behind, so that the whole city was thrown into an uproar. Among the thousands who had gone up to Jerusalem for the Passover were some from far away places who had never heard anything about Jesus. So they asked, "Who is He?"

"It is the prophet Jesus, from Nazareth in Galilee," answered the people.

Some of the Pharisees in the crowd went up to Jesus and said, "Command Your followers to be quiet."

But Jesus answered, "Even if they were quiet, the stones themselves would cry out instead."

As He came closer to Jerusalem, Jesus wept and said to the city, "If only you knew what is needed for peace! Yet you cannot see it. Your enemies will destroy you, because you have not recognized that God came to save you."

That day was the first Palm Sunday.

The next day Jesus went into the temple. Now the temple was, in a special sense, the place of God's presence, although since the coming of Jesus, people have understood that God is everywhere and is not confined to a special place.

In the outer court of the temple, the Court of the Gentiles, were a number of money-changers when Jesus went there.

Jews who came from other countries were not allowed to use their own foreign coins to pay the temple taxes, nor could they buy animals for sacrifice with anything but Jewish money. This meant that they had to go to the money-changers before they could play their part in the festival.

Now the money-changers fixed a very dishonest rate of exchange and charged very high sums, even to the poorest people who could only afford the cheapest sacrifice, which was two pigeons.

Jesus was rightly very angry when He saw all the cheating and robbing that was going on within the temple areas. He overturned the money-changers' table and stalls of those who were selling pigeons, and He drove all those who were doing such business out of the temple. "My house is a house of prayer," He cried, "but you have made it a den of thieves!"

Then blind and crippled people came to Him to be healed and He healed them in the temple. The chief priests and lawyers were angry at the wonderful things he did—while, on the other hand, they had turned a blind eye to the dishonesty of the money-changers.

Some children came in and shouted praises to Jesus, the praises which they had heard others shouting along the road to Jerusalem. "Do you hear them? Listen to what they are saying," said the chief priests and lawyers to Jesus.

"Yes," answered Jesus. "Haven't you read in the scriptures, 'Out of the mouths of babies and children shall come perfect praise'?" And he left them and went with the disciples to Bethany to lodge for the night.

THE LAST SUPPER

DURING the week which began with the first Palm Sunday came the Passover festival which was celebrated all over Israel.

Jesus and His disciples, who were now in Jerusalem, were also to celebrate the festival, and the disciples asked Jesus, "Where would you like us to go to get the Passover meal ready, for we must make the arrangements?"

Jesus replied by giving special instructions to two of the disciples: "Go into the city," He said, "and a man carrying a pitcher of water will meet you. Follow him into the house which he enters, and ask the householder where the room is where I am to eat the Passover with my disciples. He will show you an upper room and it is there that you are to prepare the Passover. The rest of us will join you there."

The two disciples went and found everything as Jesus had said.

In the evening of that day, which was Thursday, Jesus and His disciples assembled in the upper room. They did not know it then, but this was to be no ordinary Passover meal; Jesus was about to transform it into the Lord's Supper—a meal which has been continued in the Christian Church all over the world ever since.

When the supper had been served, Jesus rose from the table, took off His outer garment, and tied a towel round His waist.

130

Then He poured water into a basin and did the job which was normally performed by a slave—He began to wash the disciples' feet.

Not long before, the disciples had been arguing as to who was the greatest, and it seems that not one of them had wanted to do the menial act of feet-washing at the supper for fear of being thought less important than the others. So when Jesus saw that none of them offered to do this courteous act, He rose and willingly did it Himself for the whole company.

When He came to Simon Peter, that disciple protested, "You shall never wash my feet, Lord. It is not right."

"If I don't," said Jesus, "you have no part with me."

Jesus meant this symbolically—that unless He washed Peter's sins from him, then he had no link with Jesus.

Then Peter, perhaps beginning to understand, said, "Lord, not only my feet, but also my hands and my head."

When Jesus had washed all the disciples' feet, He returned to His place at the table and sat down facing them all.

Then He said, "You call me teacher and Lord, and you are right to do so, for that is what I am. But if I, your Lord and teacher, have washed your feet, so ought you to follow my example and wash one another's feet."

Again He was teaching them that the truly great people are those who do not put themselves first, but who serve others and do not think only of their own needs.

As they were eating, Jesus said something startling. "I tell you truly," He said, "that one of you will betray me."

The disciples were puzzled and looked at one another in alarm, each thinking, "Surely He cannot mean me." Peter motioned to the disciple who was sitting next to Jesus (most likely John) to ask Him whom he meant. The disciple asked Him quietly and Jesus replied, "It is the one to whom I give a piece of bread which I have dipped in the sauce of this dish."

Then He took a piece of bread, dipped it, and gave it to Judas Iscariot. It was Jesus's last appeal to Judas, but Judas rejected it.

"Do quickly what you are about to do," said Jesus to Judas, and again the disciples did not understand what Jesus meant, for they did not know that Judas was going to betray their master. Some of them thought that, since Judas was in charge of the money, Jesus was telling him to go out and buy what they needed for the festival, or give some money to the poor.

But Judas, after he accepted the bread from Jesus, got up and went out into the night through the dark streets of the city.

During the meal, Jesus did something wonderful. He took a piece of bread, said a prayer of thanks, broke the bread and gave it to His disciples saying, "Take and eat; this is My body which is given for you."

Then He took a cup of wine, gave thanks to God, and handed it to them saying, "This is My blood which is poured out for many for the forgiveness of sins. Do this in memory of Me."

After Judas had left, Jesus spoke again to the disciples and tried to help them to understand why His death had to happen. "I shall not be with you for very much longer," He said, "and you cannot come where I am going. Now I give you a new commandment, that you love one another. If you act in this way, then everyone will know that you are my disciples."

"Why can't I follow You now?" asked Peter. "I am ready to die for you."

"Are you?" said Jesus sadly. "I tell you that before the cock crows, you will have said three times that you did not know Me."

"I'll never say that," said Peter stoutly, "even if I have to die with You."

And the other disciples said the same, protesting their loyalty to Jesus.

Jesus told them much else about what was to happen. He would be returning to His Father and preparing the way for others to come to Him too. His return to God would bring them new power through the Holy spirit; and the Holy Spirit would be with them all the time all over the world wherever they went, not limited to one particular place, as Jesus in human form had been.

Ever since that night Christians have held the service of the Lord's Supper as Holy Communion in memory of that last meal which Jesus ate with his disciples. This service is held on both weekdays and Sundays throughout the year.

THE GARDEN OF GETHSEMANE

Now Judas was the treasurer of the little band of Jesus's disciples and therefore had charge of the money. He had not always been honest and had at times helped himself from the money bag. Yet for nearly three years he had been among the group of Jesus's closest followers, listening to Him, watching His wonderful deeds, and learning from Him. It was sad that he did not live up to Jesus's hopes for him when He first called him to be a disciple.

Some time before the Last Supper, Judas had gone to the chief priests and had asked, "How much will you give me If I betray Jesus to you?"

"Thirty silver coins," they said.

From that time Judas kept on the lookout for an opportunity to betray his master. The chief priests and elders wanted Jesus arrested secretly, for they feared that if they took Him openly, there would be a riot among the people.

When the Passover meal, that Last Supper, ended, Jesus and the disciples sang a hymn and went to the Garden of Gethsemane, which was near the foot of the slopes of the Mount of Olives. It was a quiet garden, away from the noise and bustle of Jerusalem.

Here Jesus said to eight of the disciples, "Sit here while I go over there and pray." Then He took Peter, James and John on a little further. To these three He said, "Wait here and keep watch with Me; for the sorrow in My heart is very great."

He Himself went on a short distance further and threw Himself face down on the ground and prayed to God, "Father, if it is possible, take this cup of suffering away from me; nevertheless, let not what I wish happen here, but what You wish." And God sent Him the strength to go through with what was to happen.

Then He got up and went back to the three disciples, and found that they had fallen asleep, for they were tired and worn out by grief and worry. Jesus said to Peter, "Weren't you able to keep watch with me for even one hour?" Watch and pray that you do not fall into temptation. The spirit is willing, but the flesh is weak."

Jesus went back and prayed, and again when He returned, He found the disciples had fallen asleep, for they could not keep their eyes open. He went away and prayed a third time, and found the disciples sleeping once more when He came back to them. "Are you still sleeping and resting?" He said. "Look, the time has come for the Son of Man to be given over into the hands of wicked men. Rise up! Let us be going, for the man who is to betray Me is here."

While Jesus was still speaking, a crowd of soldiers and other people, including some temple guards, came into the garden. The chief priests and elders had sent them, and they were all armed with swords and clubs and carried lanterns.

Among them was Judas. He had given them a signal, saying, "The man I kiss is the one you are after. Go up and seize Him and lead Him away safely."

Judas said to Jesus, "Hail, master!" and kissed Him.

"Do you betray the son of Man with a kiss, Judas?" asked Jesus. Then He stepped forward and asked the soldiers, "Whom do you seek?"

"Jesus of Nazareth," they answered.

"I am He," replied Jesus.

Then Simon Peter, who had a sword with him, drew it and struck one of the high priest's servants. His name was Malchus, and the blow cut off his right ear.

"Enough of that!" said Jesus to Peter, and He touched Malchus's ear and healed it. "Put your sword away. Do you think I will not drink the cup of suffering which My Father has given Me? Do not harm them."

Jesus then turned to the soldiers and chief priests and said, "Did you have to come out to fetch Me with swords and clubs as though I were a robber? I was with you in the temple day after day, and yet you did not arrest Me there. This is the hour you act, when the power of darkness rules."

And the disciples all deserted their master and ran away.

Then the soldiers and the temple guards took hold of Jesus, bound Him and took Him to the house of Annas who was the father-in-law of Caiaphas, the High Priest that year, and a very influential man. He questioned Jesus about His disciples and His teaching and all the things He had done which had angered the high priests.

While this was going on, Simon Peter had been troubled in his conscience about forsaking Jesus, and he had secretly followed Him. He went into the courtyard of the High Priest's house, and the girl who kept the door said to him, "Aren't you one of that man's disciples?"

"No," said Peter, "I am not. I don't even know Him."

It was a cold night and so the servants and guards had made a charcoal fire and were standing by it and trying to get warm. Peter went over and stood with them.

Meanwhile Jesus was still being questioned, and Annas was trying to trap Him into saying that He had started a secret society. "I have always spoken openly," said Jesus to Annas. "I taught in the synagogues and in the temple, where the Jews meet together. I said nothing secretly. Why don't you ask those who heard Me? They know what I said."

At this, one of the guards standing by struck Jesus with his hand. "How dare You speak so?" he said.

Jesus replied, "If I have said anything wrong, tell Me, but if I have not, why do you hit Me?"

Then Annas sent Him, still bound, to Caiaphas.

Peter was still standing in the courtyard warming himself, and one of those present said, "Aren't you one of that man's disciples? After all, your speech gives you away as a Galilean."

"I am not," said Peter again.

Then one of the servants of the High Priest spoke up (He was a relative of the man whose ear Peter had cut off.) "Did I not see you in the garden with Him?" he asked.

Again Peter answered, "No", and immediately the sound of a cock crowing was heard. And Peter remembered how Jesus had said to him, "Before the cock crows, you will deny Me three times." Then he went away and wept bitterly.

JESUS IS TRIED
AND CRUCIFIED

JESUS was taken that night into the house of Caiaphas, the High Priest, where all the lawyers and elders had gathered together. They did their best to find some false evidence against Jesus so that they could have Him put to death; but they were unable to find any, even though many of the "witnesses" did not tell the truth at all, but made things up and twisted the facts of real events.

Jesus kept silent, and it was not until Caiaphas asked, "Are You the Messiah, the Son of God?" that Jesus replied, "You have said so. I tell you all that you will see the Son of Man sitting at the right hand of God and coming on the clouds of heaven."

"Blasphemy!" shrieked the High Priest in furious anger. "We don't need any more witnesses. You have just heard what He said. What do you think of that?"

"He is guilty and must die," they replied full of rage and revenge.

Early the next morning the chief priests and elders completed their plans to have Jesus put to death. They bound Him in chains and handed Him over to Pilate, the Roman governor who was Caesar's representative in those parts.

When Pilate saw Jesus before him, he asked, "Are You the King of the Jews?"

"So you have said," replied Jesus, but when the chief priests and elders made further accusations against Him, He did not answer, but stood in silence before them.

"Do You hear all these things of which they are accusing You?" asked Pilate.

But when Jesus, with quiet dignity, still refused to answer, Pilate was amazed. "I find no reason to codemn this man," he said.

"His teaching is starting a riot," the accusers urged. "It began in Galilee and now He has come here."

When Pilate heard that Jesus was a Galilean, and from the region ruled by Herod, he saw a way out of his difficulty. Herod was in Jerusalem at the time, for the Passover, and so Pilate sent Jesus to him.

Now Herod had been wanting to see Jesus for some time; he had heard about His miracles and hoped to see Him perform one. So he asked Jesus many questions, but still Jesus refused to answer and Herod grew angry. He was not accustomed to such defiance.

Then the chief priests and lawyers made all sorts of accusations against Him, and the soldiers mocked Him. Contemptuously, they put a fine robe on Him and returned Him to Pilate again for his judgment.

At every Passover time it was the custom for the governor to set free one prisoner—whichever one the crowds asked for, and at that time a notorious bandit named Barabbas was being held who was sure to be put to death for his crimes.

When the crowd gathered together, Pilate saw an opportunity to free Jesus. "Which prisoner shall I set free?" he asked the assembly, "Jesus or Barabbas?"

"Barabbas!" shouted the crowd, for the chief priests and elders had been about among the people persuading them to ask for Barabbas although they knew what a bad man he was.

"What shall I do with Jesus then?" asked Pilate.

"Crucify Him," they cried.

"But what crime has He committed?" asked Pilate, and for answer they shouted all the more, "Crucify Him!"

While all this was going on, Pilate's wife sent him a message saying, "Have nothing to do with this just man; I suffered much in a dream last night because of Him."

She may have realized that Jesus was no ordinary religious teacher, and that her husband would be doing a great wrong if he allowed such an obviously innocent man to be killed. But Pilate saw there was little use in continuing to hope that Jesus might be freed, and as a sign that he was having nothing to do with it, he took a bowl of water and washed his hands in front of them all. "I am not responsible for this man's death," he said. "It is your doing."

So Barabbas was freed and Jesus was whipped and handed over to be crucified. Pilate's soldiers mocked Him, stripped off His clothes and put a purple robe on Him. Then they made a crown of thorns and put it on His head, and placed a reed in his hand. "Hail, King of the Jews!" they shouted, and struck Him and spat on Him. It was brutal behaviour.

Once more Pilate tried to reason with the crowd; he took Jesus out to them, hoping perhaps that they would take pity on Him. "Look at Him," said Pilate, in desperation, "I cannot find any reason to condemn Him!"

But still the crowds shouted, "Crucify Him! Crucify Him!"
Take Him yourselves and crucify Him," said Pilate.

"Our law says He ought to die because He claimed to be the
Son of God", shouted someone, and everyone else roared in
agreement.

This made Pilate afraid and he took Jesus aside and questioned
Him again, but still Jesus would not reply. "You know that I
have the power to set You free or to have You crucified?" said
Pilate, and this time Jesus did reply. He said, "You only have
power over Me because it was given to you by God Himself."

Then the crowd shouted to Pilate, "If you set this man free,
you're no friend of Caesar's." That was enough for Pilate. He
greatly feared the emperor and so he handed Jesus over to the
crowds to be crucified.

Crucifixion was a most horrible form of death. The victim was
nailed to a cross and left hanging there to die in agony. He also
had to carry his own cross to the site.

As Jesus was being led to the hill of Calvary, outside the city
wall, He fainted under the weight of His cross, and a man named
Simon from Cyrene was forced by the soldiers to carry it for Him
to the place of execution.

Jesus was hung between two thieves who were also crucified.
Above His head Pilate had had a notice placed reading, "Jesus of
Nazareth, King of the Jews."

Jesus was on the cross for six hours, and during that time He
spoke seven times.

First He prayed for the people and the soldiers saying,
"Father, forgive them for they do not know what they are
doing."

Then He spoke to one of the thieves who was repenting of his past, saying, "Truly I say to you today you will be with Me in Paradise."

Then He placed His mother Mary in the care of His disciple John: "Woman, behold your son! Behold your mother!"

Next, in great agony He repeated some words from a psalm, "My God, My God, why hast Thou forsaken Me?"

Then He said, "I thirst", and a sponge soaked in cheap wine was passed up to Him, after which He said, "It is finished."

Finally, He prayed, "Father, into Thy hands I commit My spirit," and then He died.

For the last three hours that Jesus was on the cross, the sun ceased to shine and there was darkness over all the land; also the curtain which hung in the temple was torn in two.

When Jesus had died, one of the soldiers plunged his spear into His side to make certain He was dead. The people who had gathered there went back home, many feeling very sad, especially those who had known Jesus personally and who were still loyal to him.

Among those who remained loyal to Jesus were two important men who wished to see that He had a proper burial. One man was named Joseph and came from Arimathea in Judea; although he was a member of the council, he had not agreed with their decision over Jesus. The other was a man named Nicodemus, who had come to Jesus one night to talk about the Kingdom of God and learn more about Jesus's way of life.

Joseph went to Pilate and asked if he could have Jesus's body. Pilate agreed, and with Nicodemus, Joseph took the body to a tomb cut in a rock in his own garden, which he had prepared for

"Jairus's little daughter would answer, 'Yes, I am sure He
will come back' ."

"John said to Peter under his breath, 'It is the Lord'."

himself. Nicodemus brought costly spices with which to anoint the body, as was the custom, and they wrapped it in linen and laid it in the tomb. Then they placed a large heavy stone over the entrance.

Mary Magdalene, one of Jesus's followers, and another woman called Mary were watching and they saw where the body of Jesus was lain and went to tell the disciples.

So ended the first Good Friday.

The next day some of the Pharisees and chief priests went to Pilate and said, "We remember that this man Jesus said He would rise again in three days. Will you give orders that the tomb is guarded until the third day, so that His disciples don't steal the body and tell people He has risen? They could cause a great deal of trouble."

"Take a guard and make the tomb as secure as possible," said Pilate.

So they went and put a seal over the stone entrance and left it guarded by Roman soldiers, both by day and by night.

THE FIRST EASTER DAY

THE day after Jesus's crucifixion was the seventh day of the week, the Jewish Sabbath (Saturday) when work was forbidden. The following day was the first day of the week (Sunday).

Very early on the morning of that day, before it was properly light, Mary Magdalene and the women who had been loyal to Jesus to the end, went to the tomb taking some sweet-smelling spices for His body.

On the way they remembered the huge stone which had been rolled across the entrance to the tomb and realized that they would probably be unable to move it. "Who will roll away the stone for us?" they wondered.

As they got nearer, however, they saw to their surprise that the stone had already been moved. St Matthew's Gospel tells us that there had been a violent earthquake, and that an angel had come down and rolled the stone away; the guards had trembled with fear and had "become like dead men".

The women crept up to the tomb and looked inside—the body of Jesus had gone! Where He had been lying stood two angels in shining white, who spoke to the women who were frightened and bowed their faces to the ground. "Don't be afraid," said the angels. "Why are you looking for the living among the dead? Jesus is not here. He has risen. You remember that He told you

146

when He was in Galilee that He would be crucified but would rise again on the third day. Go and tell His disciples, and Peter, that He is going before you into Galilee, and there you will see Him.'

Trembling with fear and astonishment, the women ran back to Jerusalem to tell the disciples what had happened. But the disciples didn't believe them and thought that they were talking nonsense.

However, Peter and John decided after a while that they had better go and see for themselves, and so they both ran off to the tomb. Now John was younger than Peter, and so he could run faster and he got there first. He stooped down and looked inside the tomb. Certainly Jesus's body was not there, but the grave-clothes were there, with the cloth which had been around Jesus's head lying separately. Obviously no one would have hurriedly taken off the grave-clothes in order to take Jesus's body away. It was as though the body had simply miraculously passed through them.

Then up came Peter, and he went straight into the tomb. John followed him—and they saw and believed, but still did not understand just what had happened. Feeling very puzzled, they returned to their homes.

Mary Magdalene had gone back to the tomb, and stood outside it weeping. She too looked inside, perhaps wondering if her eyes had deceived her the first time she had looked.

This time there were two angels sitting where the body of Jesus had been—one at the head and the other at the feet. They asked her, "Why are you weeping?"

Mary replied, "Because they have taken away my Lord, and I do not know where they have put Him."

As she said this, she turned and saw someone standing there. It was still not properly light and her eyes were blurred with tears, and so she could not see clearly who it was. "Woman, why are you weeping? Who is it that you are looking for?" the figure asked.

Thinking that it was probably the gardener who was speaking to her, Mary said, "Sir, if you have taken Him, tell me where you have laid Him, and I will take Him away."

Then He said, "Mary!" , and Mary knew it was Jesus! No one else said "Mary" just like that!

"Teacher!" she said to Him.

"Don't touch Me," said Jesus, "for I have not yet gone back to My Father; but go tell My brothers that I am returning to My Father and their Father, to My God and their God."

Joyfully Mary went to the disciples to tell them the exciting news. She had seen Jesus! And she told them all that He had said.

Meanwhile the soldiers who had been set to guard Jesus's tomb were terrified and completely baffled at what had happened. They decided that the best thing to do was to go and tell the chief priests just what had occurred—so far as they were able.

The chief priests and elders met, no doubt extremely worried, and decided that they had better try and cover up as best they could. So they gave the soldiers some money and said, "You must say that Jesus's disciples came in the night and stole His body while you were asleep. If it gets to the governor's ears, we will tell him it wasn't your fault. Don't worry."

No group of people could have been more miserable and dispirited than the disciples had been when Jesus had died. With their leader gone, they felt that all He had stood for, and all that they had worked for, was now lost. They were without hope, very sad and very afraid.

Peter especially was completely wretched, remembering how he had denied his Lord. How marvellous then to hear that special message which the angels had given to the women! "Tell His disciples, *and Peter*, that He is going before you into Galilee."

The Bible does not tell us what happened when Peter met Jesus again. No doubt this was something which Peter would want to keep to himself for ever. But we do know that Jesus did appear to Peter.

Since the wonderful event of Jesus's resurrection, upon which the Christian religion places its firm foundation, Christians have changed their main day of worship from the seventh day of the week (Saturday) to the first day (Sunday), as a reminder that the resurrection happened on a Sunday, the first day of the week.

HE IS RISEN!

LATER on, towards the evening of that wonderful first Easter day, two of Jesus's followers were walking from Jerusalem to the little village of Emmaus, a distance of about seven miles.

They did not know that Jesus had risen from the dead, though they had been hearing some strange rumours, and they talked together about the recent and terrible happenings in Jerusalem. How sad that Jesus, their friend and leader, had been put to death! It was the end of their hopes.

As they talked, Jesus Himself came up and walked along with them, but they did not recognize Him. Perhaps His appearance had changed somewhat at His resurrection, or He may have prevented their knowing Him. Certainly they would not be expecting to see Him.

"What are you talking about? What makes you look so unhappy?" asked Jesus.

They stood still, looking very sad. Then one of then, named Cleopas, said, "You must be the only visitor to Jerusalem who does not know about all the things that have been happening there during the past few days."

"What things?" asked Jesus.

"About Jesus of Nazareth, who was a wonderful prophet, mighty in deed and word," they answered. "The chief priests and rulers of the people had Him condemned to death, and He was crucified three days ago. We had hoped that He was the one, promised in the scriptures, who was going to set Israel free.

"But then there was a very surprising report. Some women went to His tomb this morning and could not find His body. They came back and said that they had seen angels who had told them that Jesus was alive. Then some others went to the tomb and found it as the women had said. But they did not see Jesus."

"O foolish men, slow to believe all that the prophets foretold," said Jesus. "Ought not the Messiah to have suffered these things and to have entered into His glory?"

Then, beginning with the laws of Moses and the writings of the prophets, Jesus explained to them what had been said about Himself in the scriptures. Cleopas and his companion must have found it hard to understand.

By this time, they were approaching the village of Emmaus, and it seemed as though Jesus intended to go on further. But, as it was getting dark, the two followers held Him back and said, "Stay with us, for it is almost dark and the day has nearly gone."

Jesus accepted their kind invitation and went in to stay and have a meal with them. As they began to eat, Jesus took some bread, blessed it, broke it into pieces and gave it to them.

Suddenly they realized who He was! Perhaps it was the words He spoke as He blessed the bread which seemed familiar to them, or they may have looked closely at His hand as He broke it and seen the marks of the nails. Whatever it was, they knew now, without doubt, that this was Jesus. Then when they looked again, He had gone!

They turned to one another and said, "We should have known!

Didn't it seem like fire burning in us while He was talking to us on the road?"

Although it was late, they got up at once and hurried all the way back to Jerusalem to tell the disciples the great news.

Some time after this, seven of the disciples were by the Sea of Galilee. The seven were Simon Peter, James and John, Thomas, Nathanael, and two others. Simon Peter said, "I'm going fishing."

"We'll come too," said the others, and they all set out.

Although the disciples worked hard all night, they did not catch any fish. Usually it was easier to catch fish at night, because they could not see the nets, but the fishermen had no success on this night.

As dawn broke and the sun began to rise, they noticed someone standing by the water's edge. "Young men," He called, "have you caught any fish?"

"Not one," they answered.

"Let your net down over the right side of the boat, and then you will catch some," advised the man.

So, despite their unsuccessful and tiring night, they threw the net out as instructed, and to their amazement found that they could not pull it back in because they had caught so many fish.

John then realized who the man on the shore was. "It is the Lord!" he gasped.

As soon as Peter heard that, he wrapped his coat around him, jumped out of the boat and waded ashore, for they were only about 100 yards from the land. The other disciples followed in the boat, dragging the net, heavy with the catch.

As they got nearer, they saw that Jesus had prepared a charcoal fire and had some fish and bread ready for them. "Bring some of those fish you've just caught," He said.

Peter went to help drag in the net and, when they counted, they found that they had caught 153 large fish; yet, much to their surprise and relief, the net was not broken, despite the great weight it held.

"Come and eat," said Jesus, and He gave them the bread and fish.

When they had eaten, Jesus said to Simon Peter, "Simon, do you love me more than these others?"

Peter had earlier boasted of his great love and loyalty for Jesus, but now, after his denials, he was more humble. "Lord, You know that I love You," he replied.

"Take care of My lambs," said Jesus, meaning His followers.

Then a second time Jesus asked Peter if he loved Him. "Yes, Lord, You know that I do," said Peter.

"Take care of My sheep," said Jesus.

A third time Jesus asked the same question, and Peter said, "Lord, you know everything. You know I love You."

"Take care of My sheep," said Jesus again.

This would not be an easy task, but Peter was to stick to it and help many "sheep" to come to love and work for Jesus, the Good Shepherd.

Peter was sad that Jesus had asked him three times if he loved Him, but as he had once denied Jesus three times, perhaps this was Jesus's way of cancelling out these three denials with the three statements that Peter really did love Him. It was also a way of restoring Peter to his old position as leader, and of giving him the task of caring for people.

THE ASCENSION
AND FIRST WHITSUNDAY

FOR forty days after Jesus had risen from the dead on the first Easter Sunday, He was seen by many of His friends at various times. There could be no doubt that He was alive again and had risen from the dead, just as He had said He would.

Sometimes He was with them, sometimes He was not. He could appear among them even if they were in a room with all the doors and windows firmly closed, for His body was different since His resurrection.

When He came in the midst of them like that He always knew what had been happening just beforehand. Gradually they began to realize that whether they could see Him or not, whether they could hear Him or not, He was always with them and this gave them great comfort.

During this time—sometimes referred to as the 'Great Forty Days'—the disciples listened hard to what He told them, learning no doubt that they would be expected to carry on His work. For He knew that the time was coming when He would have to leave them in bodily form, and they would not actually see and hear Him on earth any more as they had until now.

He charged the disciples: "Go into all the world and make people My disciples, baptizing them in the name of the Father, and of the Son, and of the Holy Spirit, and teaching them to obey

My commands. And I will be with you always, even until the end of the world."

Now on the fortieth day after the resurrection, He had led them out as far as Bethany and on to a hill. He had given them special orders that they were not to leave Jerusalem until they received the gift of the Holy Spirit which would strengthen them for their great work and give them the courage they would need.

"Are You now going to restore Israel to be a great nation again?" asked the disciples. They hoped He would make the Jewish nation independent of Rome, which was what the Jews had always thought the Messiah would do. They still had not learned that God's Kingdom is not of this world. After all, if He who had been killed and had then risen from the dead were to show Himself to all the people in Jerusalem and to the chief priests and elders and to Pilate and King Herod, surely then they would have to accept that He was truly the Messiah, the Son of God, King of the Jews.

"It is not for anyone to know that," said Jesus, "for times and seasons belong to God's authority alone."

Meanwhile the disciples had to set about the task of winning the world for God—a seemingly impossible job for such a small band of men, but Jesus knew that with God all things are possible, and He said, "When the Holy Spirit comes to you, you will be filled with power and will be My witnesses in Jerusalem, in all Judea and Samaria, and to the ends of the earth."

After He had said this, He blessed them, and then a cloud covered Him and took Him up out of their sight.

As the disciples stood gazing at the sky, two angels appeared beside them and said, "You men of Galilee, why are you standing gazing up into heaven? This same Jesus, who was taken from you into heaven, will come back in the same way that you have seen Him depart from you into heaven."

Although the disciples would see Jesus no more, they felt happy and returned to Jerusalem with great joy. They were happy because He had blessed them, and full of joy that He would always be with them, even though they could not see Him any longer as they had done before.

Now they could look forward to the coming of God's Holy Spirit which would give them power and strength for the great work which was ahead.

The day on which Jesus ascended to heaven is called Ascension Day, and it is celebrated by the Church each year on the fortieth day after Easter (always on a Thursday).

"Ascension" means "going up". When we say that Jesus "ascended to heaven", we do not necessarily mean that heaven is a place above the sky. "Up" in this sense means "better, different", rather as you might say you were "going up" in school, even though your new classroom may be on a lower floor than your previous one.

After Jesus's ascension into heaven, the disciples went back to Jerusalem. They were still afraid of the Jewish authorities who had killed Jesus, so they stayed indoors where they felt safer. Each day after the ascension they wondered if the gift of the Holy Spirit would come that day and they watched and waited.

A week went by, then eight days, nine days, and, at last, on the tenth day something strange and wonderful happened.

Now the tenth day happened to be the feast of Pentecost. Pentecost means "fifty", and this feast always came fifty days after the Passover. Pentecost marked the end of the barley harvest, when the Jews presented freshly baked loaves of new, fine, leavened flour in the temple. It was a day of rejoicing and gratitude for the gifts of the earth—rather like a harvest festival. Many people from many countries came to Jerusalem to take part in the feast of Pentecost. It was always a very happy and busy time in the city.

Jesus's band of inner disciples now numbered twelve again, for a new man named Matthias had been chosen to replace Judas Iscariot who had killed himself after his evil deed of betrayal on that night in the Garden of Gethsemane.

This band of twelve are known as the twelve apostles—the word "apostle" means "one who is sent" (to preach and teach). The word "disciple" means "learner"—and all those who followed Jesus, believed in Him and wanted to obey His teachings were considered as disciples, including the apostles.

On this day of Pentecost, the apostles and probably some other disciples were all gathered together in one place.

Suddenly there was a loud noise, like a rushing mighty wind, and it filled the whole house where they were sitting. They looked at one another in astonishment and saw a glowing light split up into what looked like flames of fire hovering above each of their heads. This was the outward sign that the promised gift of God's Holy Spirit had now come to them.

The mighty wind was a symbol of the power and energy of the Holy Spirit, and the flames of fire were a symbol of the fiery zeal with which the disciples would now be able to proclaim the Gospel.

The effect on them was tremendous. No longer were they

weak, cowering, frightened people; instead they felt strong and brave and were filled with a great strength. They found, too, that they could do things which they had been unable to do before. When they spoke to the crowds a little later, they discovered that people who did not speak their language could still understand what they said.

The disciples felt filled with such courage and strength that they immediately left the house and went among the crowds of people outside. These included not only those who lived in Jerusalem, but also countless visitors who had come to Jerusalem for the feast of Pentecost. There were Parthians, Medes and Elamites, representing countries from beyond the influence of the Roman Empire; there were people from Mesopotamia, from Judea, from Cappadocia, Asia Minor, Pamphylia, Egypt and Libya, Crete and Arabia. Yet they could all understand what the disciples were telling them about the wonderful and mighty works of God.

Normally the Galilean speech of the disciples would not have been easy to follow. Now everyone in the crowd heard his own language being spoken. They were amazed and puzzled.

"What does it mean?" the crowds asked one another. "They are drunk with wine," said others mockingly.

Then Peter, standing up with the other eleven apostles, began to speak courageously to the crowd in a loud voice. It was the first ever Christian sermon. "These people are not drunk with wine," he began, "but what you see and hear is what the prophet Joel said would happen. He said that God would send His Spirit to all." (Peter was quoting from the prophet Joel whose book forms part of the Old Testament.)

"Listen to these words, men of Israel," went on Peter, "Jesus of Nazareth was sent by God—a fact proved by all the wonders and miracles which God worked through Him. Yet by the hands of sinful and lawless men He was crucified. But God raised Him from the dead, and set Him free from the power of death. Moreover, He has ascended to the right hand of God, and has sent His Holy Spirit as He promised. What you now see and hear is that gift of the Holy Spirit which is poured out upon us. It is certain that this Jesus, whom you crucified, is the One whom God has sent to be our Lord and Messiah."

When the people heard this brave message, many of them were upset and very troubled. They said to the apostles, "What shall we do then?"

Peter replied, "You must start afresh. Give up your sins and be baptized in the name of Jesus Christ. Your sins will then be forgiven, and you will receive the gift of the Holy Spirit."

Many of the crowd believed Peter's powerful words and they came to be baptized. About 3,000 people were added to the group of believers on that day. They learnt from the apostles and shared fellowship meals and prayer.

Because of their firm faith, the apostles were able to perform many miracles and wonders, and more and more believers were added to their number. Baptism was followed by a new sense of community, which resulted in a practical sharing of their belongings with one another. The richer ones among them sold their property and possessions and gave the money to those who were in need. Every day they went to the temple, and had meals together in their homes. Thus began the Christian Church on the first Whitsunday.